25.9.98.

DEVELOPING SERVICES FOR YOU

£11·95

GW01260416

DEVELOPING SERVICES FOR YOUNG PEOPLE IN CRISIS

Edited by John Dennington
and John Pitts

LONGMAN

Published by Longman Group UK Limited
6th Floor, Westgate House, The High, Harlow, Essex CM20 1YR
Telephone (0279) 442601
Telex 81491 Padlog
Fax (0279) 444501

© Longman Group UK Limited, 1991

All rights reserved. No part of this publication may be
reproduced, stored in a retrieval system, or transmitted in any form or by any
means, electronic, mechanical, photocopying, recording or otherwise, without either the prior written permission of the Publishers or a
licence permitting restricted copying issued by the Copyright Licensing
Agency Ltd, 90 Tottenham Court Road, London, WIP 9HE

First published 1991

British Library Cataloguing in Publication Data
A catalogue record for this book is available from the British Library.

ISBN 0-582-08691-4

Produced by Longman Group (F.E.) Ltd
Printed in Hong Kong

This book is dedicated to troublesome people everywhere

Acknowledgements

Many people have contributed to the work which is recorded in this book. Social workers discussed the issues in their team meetings and young people discussed them with their social workers and social work students. Social workers, managers and foster parents attended the open forums and allowed us to overhear them and use their ideas. For that, and all the support they gave us, we thank them.

Shirley Hixon offered administrative support throughout and dealt with each new crisis calmly and with enviable good humour. The staff from the Director's office pulled out the stops in helping to prepare the manuscript in time for deadlines. Chris Stanley from NACRO and David Crimmens from the Children's Society Central London Teenage Project offered us new perspectives and some refreshing objectivity. Philip Smith planned, organised and chaired the open forums with panache. Julie Jones held things together and kept them moving in an unobtrusive but very effective way and Matthew Pitts did something remarkable with a computer when we really needed it. Our sincere thanks to them all.

From the beginning, Alan Dearling, the commissioning editor, offered us support, advice and encouragement. That this book has seen the light of day is due in no small part to the commitment of Alan and John Harper at Longman.

John Dennington and John Pitts   January 1991

Contents

Acknowledgements	vi
Contributors	viii
Foreword	x
David Whitehouse	
1 Less harm or more good? Politics, research and practice with young people in crisis *John Pitts*	1
2 Creating choices. Working with long-term solvent abusers *John Kilfeather and Viv Parker*	15
3• Breaking the silence: developing work with abused young people in care *Lydia Ball, William Chatterton, Marie Clarke, Josephine Cullen, Rachael Hetherington, John Kane, Chris Iveson, Carol Knights, Heather Loxley, Maggie Phelan, Jill Roucroft and Robin Solomon Roychowdhury*	37
4 Preparation for poverty: Rethinking residential care *Mike Allin, David Barrett, Hamish Canham, Gill Harris, Nick Moore, John Pitts, Steve Tall, Rinske Taekema and Claire Walker*	56
5 The mother of invention — negative reform and secure accommodation *John Dennington*	74
6 The hard core — taking young people out of secure institutions *Cathy Aymer, Joan Gittens, Dave Hill, Ian McLeod, John Pitts, Marica Rytovaata, Eileen Sturdivant, Larry Wright and Marietta Walker*	92
7 Running out of care: developing a service for young runaways *David Crimmens*	113
8 Towards a policy for effective work with marginalised young people *Tim Bateman, John Dennington, Kath Kelly, Terry Lyons, Geoff Pick, John Pitts and Chris Stanley*	130
9 Managing change and improving services for young people in crisis *Chris Gostick*	142

Contributors

Mike Allin	Senior Day Assessment Unit Social Worker
Cathy Aymer	Principal Lecturer in Social Work at WLIHE
Lydia Ball	Field Social Worker
David Barrett	Senior Lecturer in Social Work at WLIHE
Tim Bateman	Intermediate Treatment Assessment Worker
Hamish Canham	Residential Social Worker
William Chatterton	Assistant Divisional Director, Child Protection
Marie Clarke	Assessment Foster Parent
David Crimmens	Project Leader, Central London Teenage Project
Josephine Cullen	Field Social Worker
John Dennington	Assistant Director, Children and Families
Joan Gittens	Assistant Residential Manager
Chris Gostick	Director of Social Services
Alan Hanford	Assistant Residential Manager
Gill Harris	Community Fostering Social Worker
Rachael Hetherington	Senior Lecturer in Social Work at WLIHE
Dave Hill	Residential Services Manager
Chris Iveson	Social Work Team Leader
John Kane	Intermediate Treatment Project Leader
Kath Kelly	Assistant Residential Manager
John Kilfeather	Intermediate Treatment Worker
Carol Knights	Assessment Foster Parent
Heather Loxley	Community Fostering Team Leader
Terry Lyons	Head of Assessment Services (Under 12s)
Ian McLeod	Assistant Residential Manager
Nick Moore	Residential Manager
Viv Parker	Intermediate Treatment Project Leader
Maggie Phelan	Residential Social Worker
Geoff Pick	Intermediate Treatment Manager
John Pitts	Reader in Applied Social Science at WLIHE
Jill Roucroft	Intermediate Treatment Project Leader
Robin Solomon Roychowdhury	Senior Lecturer in Social Work at WLIHE
Marica Rytovaata	Senior Social Worker, Adolescent Psychiatric Unit
Chris Stanley	Development Officer, NACRO

Contributors

Eileen Sturdivant	Courts Officer
Rinske Taekema	Assistant Residential Manager
Steve Tall	Social Work Team Leader
Clare Walker	Head of Assessment Services (Adolescents)
Marietta Walker	Assistant Residential Manager
David Whitehouse	Head of the Department of Social Work at WLIHE
Larry Wright	Intermediate Treatment Project Leader

Foreword

Today, in social work and social work education there is a growing emphasis on collaboration and partnership. This book reveals a new dimension to such collaboration by showing how a group of academic researchers, and practitioners and managers in a social work agency entered a partnership to define certain problems more clearly and to develop effective responses to those problems.

As Chris Gostick notes in the final chapter, collaborative research can generate change in organisations not simply because it yields new information but because the collaborative process itself develops momentum for change amongst participants. What is true for social work agencies is also true for academic departments. The work described in this book has added a new dimension to the work of the Social Work Department at the West London Institute. As teachers we talk a lot about change but this has been an opportunity to participate in the difficult and uncertain business of change. In the process, like the practitioners and managers with whom we have worked, we have had to refine and revise our ideas about what social work is and what social workers should do.

This is no simple question of reorganisation and retraining however. As ever, the process of defining what social workers should or should not do involves political choices and decisions about the deployment of resources. But these choices should also reflect the real needs and real problems experienced by socially disadvantaged people. Yet, all too often, the debate about the future of social work is conducted with scant reference to its actual and potential clientelle.

This book is about developing services for, and with, a group of people whose voices are seldom heard and whose needs are all too often ignored; young people in crisis. Indeed the past decade has seen a steady deterioration in the already critical predicament of our most vulnerable young people. A large number of young homeless people in London have been 'released' from psychiatric hospitals or discharged from local authority care or custody. Their predicament reflects the absence of any effective network of support and the paucity of work and housing. It is compounded by changes in the rules governing eligibility to state benefits which disadvantage these already disadvantaged young people even further.

Foreword

Developing services for young people in crisis records an attempt by social work practitioners, managers, educators and researchers to explore and develop a different kind of service. It is a service which attempts to anticipate the problems which vulnerable young people may be experiencing or may subsequently encounter. It strives to forestall those problems whose solution lies in the hands of the local authority or the voluntary sector, and to forearm young people to deal with those which do not. At one point, for example, the book asks whether residential care should be more than a 'preparation for poverty'. It proceeds to explore the minimum standards of provision and practice required to ensure that it is not.

This book is very timely. In a period when local authorities are cutting community provision for young offenders, residential child care is the subject of political debate and scrutiny, and the confidence of residential social workers is at a very low ebb, *Developing services for young people in crisis* offers us a salutary reminder that good practice is possible and that effective intervention with vulnerable young people can save both money and lives. It expresses an optimism about the possibility of positive change and offers examples of ways in which social work practitioners and managers can work together to develop modes of work which enhance rather than jeopardise the life-chances of vulnerable young people.

David Whitehouse January 1991
Head of the Social Work Department,
West London Institute of Higher Education

Something is pushing them
to the side of their own lives

Afternoons by Philip Larkin

1 Less harm or more good? Politics, research and practice with young people in crisis

John Pitts

> This chapter considers the political, theoretical and economic constraints open social services practitioners and managers in the past decade and suggests how new ways of finding out about problems can enable managers and professionals to make more 'intelligent' responses to them.

Telling stories about residential child care

Some time before embarking upon the work reported in this book my colleagues and I were discussing the state of residential child care. What we discussed, while being neither new nor uncommon, was nonetheless, we thought, theoretically interesting.

We had all listened to accounts of the operation of social services departments given by senior managers of residential services, they tended to be 'cautiously optimistic'. There were 'problems', 'of course' but, paradoxically, these 'problems' were also 'opportunities'. Cuts in resources had mobilised the creativity of staff and in consequence we had seen the emergence of a 'slimmed-down', 'tighly targetted', 'radically non-interventionist', 'value-for-money', 'non-net-widening' service. Things were being 'firmed-up' and 'buttoned down', 'gates' were being 'kept', 'challenges' were being 'met', 'bottom lines' balanced and managers were 'getting it right'.

At the other end of the hierarchy we found a lot of cynical basic grade residential workers who believed that the rhetoric of scientific management and liberal reform were being used to justify both the erosion of services to clients and the conditions for an effective professional practice. They usually wanted better, or indeed some, supervision and the time and opportunity to develop a more sophisticated practice, family therapy, behavioural techniques etc. They also suspected that research was being used by managers as a stick with which to beat social workers into an acceptance of administrative rationalisations.

The young people we spoke to, who had been recipients of these services, tended to distinguish between the good and bad places they had been and workers who had, or had not, been helpful. Places which young people thought were 'good' tended to be those which were well organised, where they felt accepted and respected but where they weren't allowed to 'get away with murder'. Interestingly one of the most helpful things that 'helpful' workers did was to cajole them into doing things that they did not want to do, like their homework. Although they wanted to be listened to and sometimes wanted to be helped they did not usually want therapy. They wanted somebody who cared about them, but they did not want to be somebody's professional case. They thought that in terms of the maintenance of buildings and consistency of staffing, residential care was getting much worse and that provision for people leaving care was wholly inadequate.

Standing conference

The work reported in this book arose out of a collaboration between the staff of the Adolescent Services Division of an inner city Social Services Department and the Social Work Department of the West London Institute of Higher Education. In 1989 the division established a Standing Conference on Adolescents which aimed to investigate:

1. the circumstances in which young people, aged 10 to 21 were selected for placement in secure units, custodial institutions, secure psychiatric facilities and 'bed and breakfast' accommodation and whether, and if so how, they might be removed from these placements;
2. the variation in the quality of residential care/fostering offered to young people;
3. the resources available for, and the adequacy and appropriateness of professional responses to, young people admitted to care who have been abused;
4. how to develop and target services for previously unreached young people, eg runaways, the young homeless, substance abusers, prostitutes etc.

The idea for a standing conference arose out of conversations about these issues between the social workers and social work managers in an inner city social services department. They in turn approached staff of the Institute of Higher Education and together approached NACRO and the Children's Society who offered to send consultants to the standing conference. It was co-ordinated by a steering group comprising representatives of each of the working groups, senior managers and a researcher from the West London Institute of Higher Education.

Staff from the Institute acted as a resource to the working groups, tracking down relevant publications and research reports, working with managers and practitioners to devise research instruments and helping to decode and write-up the results. However, much of the time was spent in clarifying the theoretical and ideological assumptions which underlay current policy and practice and devising new concepts with which to rethink issues and problems.

Students from the Institute interviewed young people and twice during the project open forums, attended by departmental staff and foster parents, were held. Here, the working groups presented their work in progress and other staff and foster parents offered criticism and suggestions for improvements. The forums offered an opportunity for a department-wide dialogue on the issues being investigated and allowed members of the directorate, managers and practitioners to ask questions of each other which they had not asked before.

The ways in which the standing conference approached its tasks were significantly different, both methodologically and theoretically, from most other research which has emanated from social services departments in the previous decade and a half. Whereas much of this research has been, as it were, visited upon social workers by outside academics contracted by social work managers, the research reported here was planned, executed and reported by social workers, social work managers and academic researchers. Whereas work in this area has tended to characterise social workers as 'zookeepers' of deviance and their clients as the hapless victims of labelling, this work represents a stage in a process of enabling young people to exert an influence on the functioning of the social services department and, in consequence, to increase the control they have over their lives.

Limitations of the labelling perspective

We started this chapter with the problem of the divergent accounts of the residential child care system; what were we to do with them? In search of an answer we considered the solution offered by Howard Becker (1967) whose work, like that of the other American social reaction or labelling theorists of the 1960s, has, to a greater or lesser extent, formed most of the significant research in juvenile justice and residential care in Britain in the past decade and a half (Thorpe et al. 1980, Morris et al. 1980, Millham et al. 1989). Becker's highly influential answer threw up some important questions however.

Becker suggests that the accounts actors give of their experience in institutions or organisations must inevitably differ in accordance with the positions they occupy in the status hierarchy. Where they stand, it seems, determines their point of view. He argues that, confronted with such divergent accounts of the world, sociologists must abandon the fruitless endeavour to pin down some abstraction called 'reality' and instead make a moral and ethical choice about 'whose side (they) are on' (see Thorpe et al. 1980). Becker's is a world of normative ghettoes, and the researcher or practitioner is destined to speak for the inhabitants of one ghetto rather than another. In Becker's view the ethical choice will require us to side with the 'underdogs', the low-power actors, the people who are least able to articulate their plight rather than their 'zookeepers'. In consequence, he maintains, we must set our faces against the MAN, the high-power actors who dominate both institutions and discourse about institutions.

While it is clearly the case that people with differential access to power in an organisation will experience that organisation differently, those engaged in applied research abandon the search for a 'total' picture at their peril. If they do attempt to put 'reality' into brackets and simply make a choice about whose side they are on, they may run into formidable difficulties. They may, for example, encounter difficulties in distinguishing between different groups of underdogs or in identifying the moment at which an underdog becomes an oppressor. Is the 19-year-old untrained, underpaid and inexperienced temporary residential worker an oppressor? Is the victim of sexual abuse who goes on to intimidate and sexually abuse fellow residents an underdog? Are the staff of a women's refuge or a 'safe house' for young runaways 'zookeepers'?

Beyond this however is the broader problem, bequeathed to us by Becker and the other labelling theorists that, contrary to the tenor of their arguments, problems in institutions are not simply solved if the activities of the 'zookeepers' who staff those institutions are neutralised. Many of the problems which afflict institutions do not originate within them. Institutions are brought into being to serve a variety of functions and social and political interests which are not determined by those who staff them (Mathiesen 1974, Pitts 1988). As a result, managers, practitioners and residents may, and often do, find themselves in agreement about what is wrong and what needs to be changed. What they lack is a means of effecting such change.

Given these problems, we wondered why the solutions offered by Becker and the other labelling theorists had held such sway for so long with perfectly respectable, indeed eminent, researchers working in this area, when they were so problematic for us. The answer to this question came gradually; whereas our research concerned the development of 'what ought to be', theirs was concerned to eliminate 'what ought not to be'. We were concerned, in part at least, with intervention, they with non-intervention. In consequence, while we were pre-occupied with how to do 'more good', to deliver a better service, they were at pains to discover how to do 'less harm'. While we entertained conflicting accounts of reality they had chosen 'whose side (they) were on'. While the labelling theorists were primarily concerned with developing policies which limited the autonomy of welfare professionals, thus countering the tendency towards 'net-widening', we were concerned to promote policies which facilitated new forms of practice which would be used to intervene more effectively in the lives of existing institutional populations and also in the lives of entirely new, previously unreached ones as well.

Our problem, in short, was that we were trying to do the opposite of what most respectable policy-makers, administrators and researchers in this field had been doing for the preceeding decade and a half.

It would seem appropriate at this point, therefore, to take a brief, and admittedly somewhat schematic, excursion into the recent history of the relationship between social scientific theory, applied social research and managers and practitioners in the fields of offending, abused and endangered young people.

The rise of minimalism

Christopher Booker (1980) claims that the post war period, up to the mid-1970s, was characterised by, amongst other things:

> The utopian belief that, through drastic social and political reorganisation, aided by the greater use of state planning we should be able to create an entirely new kind of just, fair and equal society.

He goes on ...

> The importance of the seventies was that in each of these great avenues of human exploration, they had marked a 'moment of truth', a point at which more obviously and inescapably than ever before, the dream ran out.

Certainly, in British social work in the mid-1970s, it was becoming increasingly evident that the optimistic promise of the social policy of the 1960s which was intended to complete the work of the welfare state and usher in this 'just, fair and equal society', was not to be realised.

The tide had turned and the problem solvers had become the problem. For the radical right, social workers were simply making excuses for the bad behaviour of their clients while social welfare constituted an intolerable market imperfection. For the liberal centre they were a manifestation of the creeping totalitarianism which was eroding individual rights everywhere. For the radical left they were the velvet glove concealing the iron fist of capitalist domination; the ideological state apparatus at its most subtle.

Old alliances crumbled. In the mid-1960s it had seemed that a partnership of theorists and practitioners, sociologists and social workers, criminologists and probation officers was set to deliver a scientifically informed technology or change for the burgeoning personal social services. By the mid-1970s sociologists were accusing social workers of being 'zookeepers of deviance', stigmatising, and so projecting into deviant careers, the very populations they claimed to be helping. Criminologists announced the 'decline of the rehabilitative ideal' and told probation officers that nothing they did worked any more. Daniel Moynihan (1969) sounded the death knell of community work in his ominously titled *Maximum Feasible Misunderstanding*.

By the late 1970s theorists, researchers and policy-makers working in social welfare, drawing on the work of the labelling theorists had shifted the object of research and intervention away from the individual, group or neighbourhood towards the (mal) functioning of the social welfare system itself. Rather than the behaviour of clients, now it was the operation of stigmatising professional and administrative interventions which were problematic.

Radical non-intervention

This changed orientation found its clearest expression in Shur's idea of *radical non-intervention* (1974). Shur enjoined us, whenever and wherever possible, to 'leave the kids alone', to leave them, as it were, to their own devices of social control. This non-interventionist critique, which focused initially on juvenile justice and psychiatry, was quickly applied to other areas. In the mid-1970s David Brandon undertook research at Centrepoint, the shelter for homeless young people in Central London. He maintained that through their preoccupation with the idea that young people who ran away from home might have problems, staff were simply pathologising the rational but unconventional choices they made, in David Thorpe's phrase. They were practising 'needology' (Thorpe et al. 1980). More recently of course we have learned that as many as 38 per cent of boys and 73 per cent of girls who run away from home have been abused (McCormack et al. 1988).

Radical non-intervention attracted many different people for many different reasons. For the political right radical non-intervention offered the possibility of the erosion of the power and autonomy of professionals and a return to common sense and just desserts (Morgan 1978). For the liberal centre, the erosion of the power and autonomy of professionals held the promise of an extension of the legal rights of the child (Morris et al. 1980). The political left reasoned that if the state could not be smashed then a bit of erosion was probably the next best thing. For hard-pressed local authority social services departments radical non-intervention allowed them simultaneously to be seen to be taking cognisance of the unintended consequences of social intervention, to demonstrate a respect for the rights of the child and to close much of their expensive residential provision.

From professionalism to managerialism

If the period from the mid-1960s to the early 1970s can be characterised as the era of *professionalism*, the period from the late 1970s to the mid-1980s could be characterised as the era of *managerialism*. In this period, 'being on the side', or acting 'in the interests' of young people came increasingly to be defined in terms of the minimisation of professional intervention in their lives. The development of professional practice came gradually to take second place to the development of policy, and social imperatives were increasingly subordinated to economic ones. As a result, interventions by managers which aimed to limit the involvement of welfare professionals in people's lives came to assume the mantle of radicalism while practitioners who insisted upon seeking out new 'needs' were portrayed as reactionaries (Thorpe et al. 1980, Morris et al. 1980).

No wonder then that social services managers were expressing optimism while social work professionals were expressing pessimism. Managers were in the forefront of progressive change, and rationing resources and serving the client's best interests were no longer necessarily contradictory. It was the basic grade practitioners, confronted by what appeared to be real needs, wanting to respond, yet knowing that the resources were not there, and fearing that even if they did respond they might be committing 'needology', who experienced the dissonance, the pessimism and the doubt.

Staff shortages ensured that social workers were increasingly forced back from face-to-face work with abusing families or young offenders to a 'case-management' on brokerage role. In this period welfare professionals in general and workers with young people in particular, came in from the 'street' and took their places in front of the VDUs or behind the one-way mirrors.

Rennaisance of punishment and control

Ironically perhaps, it was during the period when managerial radicalism came to the fore that face-to-face practice with young people became both more controlling and more punitive. The era of minimal or non-intervention was also the era in which the perceived need to exert 'control' over 'difficult' and delinquent young people infused face-to-face work. It was the era of behavioural contracts, correctional curricula, tracking, reparation and atonement. At the extreme end of these developments we saw Skynner's enormously important observation that one of the most problematic aspects of familial crises can be the anxieties of the professionals transmogrified into the practice of anaesthetising adolescents in psychiatric units when staff become anxious about them (Skynner 1971).

At one level the emergence of these technologies of containment and conformity reflected the pessimism about the possibility of effecting lasting individual or social change which afflicted both theory and practice during the period. At another level however it marked an abandonment of the idea of the perfectibility and innate goodness of human beings which had informed social theory and social policy in the late 1960s. In its place there emerged a far more pessimistic view of human beings as creatures motivated solely by the pursuit of pleasure and the avoidance of pain, which percolated down from government, the pro-government media and the, 'right-wing *intelligentsia*', from the late 1970s onwards.

The emergence of punitive and controlling methods of working can be explained neither by their effectiveness nor the ineffectiveness of alternative methods. There is, in fact, little reliable evidence about either. The fact is that tracking, correctional programmes and behavioural contracts offered an increasingly fractious juvenile bench and increasingly hard-pressed local authorities an explicitly controlling but cheap response to juvenile misbehaviour (DHSS 1983, Home Office 1990).

Beyond pessimism

In the past decade and a half, social work with young people in the care and justice systems has been characterised by a profound pessimism about the possibility of positive change or development. This has led to the emergence of minimal interventions which aim whenever and wherever possible to leave young people to their own devices. Because the assumptions which informed the standing conference were very different, it was necessary to examine the minimalist argument closely and in doing this we came upon a number of problems.

One of our criticisms of minimalism is its espousal of 'impossibilism', the insistence that nothing, no form of social intervention with young people, works (Young 1986). We criticise it because it is simply not true. Tightly-targeted social crime prevention initiatives developed in co-operation with young people have been shown to be remarkably successful. So have some residential treatment programmes, and certain types of individual and group therapy (Smith, Farrant and Marchant 1972, Bright and Petterson 1984, NACRO Youth Activities Unit 1988, King 1988, Blagg and Smith 1989).

Social crime prevention programmes also demonstrate that it is possible to intervene in offending behaviour in non-stigmatising ways and that, in consequence, the 'spreading the net' of control is not an inevitable corollary of such intervention.

Becker enjoins us to choose 'whose side we are on', and having chosen, to articulate the plight of the underdog. As we have suggested however, all too often, Becker's followers have taken a short cut, articulating what they assume to be the plight of the people they assume to be the underdogs without checking it out with them first. As a result, all to often, we find them 'telling it like it isn't', uncritically advocating the minimisation of responses to a group of people who are already bearing the brunt of cutbacks in national and local government services.

In one local authority vulnerable, sexually abused young women who are unable to survive in foster placements, when they can be found, are being placed in bed and breakfast accommodation near a large railway terminus which is the centre of prostitution in that part of the city. The workers and the young people both want a place in a children's home but they have all been shut as a result of progressive reforms. Chapter 4 of this book considers what local authorities can do to transform residential services for young people into an available option, which offers a positive choice rather than just preparation for poverty.

A few years ago workers and residents in a West London borough locked themselves into a long-stay children's home which was threatened with closure and successfully applied for a series of high court writs restraining the local authority from closing the establishment. The local authority was attempting to get out of the residential care business and into the much more cost-effective and 'humane' adolescent fostering business. The residents said that the establishment was their home, as it had indeed been for many years for most of them, and they wanted to stay there with the people with whom they had the closest relationships. Young people in a North London homelessness hostel do not want to be moved on to council flats because they enjoy the warmth and companionship of the hostel. The National Association for Young

People in Care (NAYPIC) campaigns for the rights of children and young people in care. One of those rights is consistent contact with the same social worker so that they can work on their problems if they have any.

This is not a bland defence of the residential solution but in the inner city in 1989 social workers, who five years ago were struggling to keep young people out of institutions, are today desperately looking for residential placements for vulnerable, homeless, rejected young people.

The picture is complicated and contradictory. It is generally agreed that despite substantial recent reductions we are still locking up far too many young people in secure units and custody. Chapter 5 explores how an abolitionist strategy can be adopted to remove young people from secure units while Chapter 6 discusses the conditions under which effective work in the community with these young people could be developed. Yet as we lock up one group of disadvantaged young people, we are simultaneously abandoning 15- and 16-year-old victims of abuse to the streets. In Chapter 3 the development of a programme of work with the victims of such abuse is described while in Chapter 7 David Crimmens outlines the strategy the Central London Teenage Project has developed with young people who run away from home and residential care.

The period which has seen the rise of minimalism has also witnessed an unprecedented increase in solvent and opiate abuse, teenage prostitution, youth homelessness, youth suicide, the decanting of vulnerable young psychiatric patients into what is euphemistically known as the community and the discovery of the widespread sexual abuse of young people. Chapter 2 of this book records the development of a client-led outreach programme for chronic solvent abusers and indicates that there is no contradiction, and no necessary danger of 'net-widening', in developing programmes which seek to extend contact with young people in need alongside minimalist IT programmes.

The minimalists, because they have lost contact with the disadvantaged young people on whose behalf they claim to speak, are in danger of jeopardising the interests of those young people. The problem is not to devise a new orthodoxy to replace minimalism but to devise a means whereby the real, and sometimes rapidly changing, interests of these young people might be articulated and represented.

Even when researchers did 'tell it like it is', there was never any guarantee that anybody, let alone those with the power to change the way it was, would be listening. It seems that the problem for applied research is not simply to articulate a voice but to ensure that that voice has some impact on the decisions which affect its owner. Thus we need to promote more than simple articulation, we have to empower the relatively powerless in such a dialogue.

If we were searching for underdogs then, in our book, basic grade workers in residential establishments would be serious contenders for the title. So, at times, would middle managers in social services departments. Chapter 8 explores how the ideas of practitioners and managers can be articulated and their creativity harnessed to the process of change. To approach complex social phenomena in a simplistic way produces dangerously simplistic answers. Richard Titmus warned us that 'the denial of complexity is the essence of tyranny' and so it has sometimes proved to be. To embrace the complexity of competing accounts of events is not to deny the differential power of those who give those accounts but, rather, to develop an analysis, the sophistication of which matches the complexity of the phenomenon. We therefore needed a methodology which could do this.

Dialogue as method

If our analysis was correct we needed a methodology which would enable us to bring together competing accounts of the problem in a situation in which people felt free to speak. We were conscious that the accounts we would hear would come from people in very different power positions.

We also knew that the practitioners were at best sceptical about research and that many people were tired of being PhD fodder. The practitioners were tired of their contributions to research being visited back upon them in the form of a debilitating critique which told them to make better use of the few resources they had. For their part the young people were tired of helping other people to make careers out of the fact that they had no chance of making a career for themselves.

It seemed to us that we had to develop a methodology which enabled practitioners and young people, and not just managers, to have some share in, and some control over the research. We therefore needed a methodology which enabled all parties to enter a dialogue; a process in which usually unheard voices could be heard and forgotten people remembered. In Skynner's (1974) terms we saw the need to connect the minimum sufficient network necessary to make an intelligent response to the problem. An intelligent response, in this perspective could only be made if that network included practitioners, foster parents, young people members of other youth-serving agencies, managers and policy-makers. John Herron (1981) writes:

> There are two quite different ways of interacting with people in research. One way is to interact with them so that they make no

direct contribution to formulating the propositions that purport to be about them or to be based on their sayings or doings ...

The other way — the way of co-operative inquiry — is for the researcher to interact with the subjects so that they do contribute directly both to hypothesis-making, to formulating the final conclusion, and to what goes on in between.

Our research aimed to reconnect the disconnected parts of the system. Rather than people at different levels simply 'telling it like it is' from their point of view, they were to be connected to a dialogue, a process of learning, change and development which connects parties whose interests may be in conflict. One of the benefits of such dialogue is that by articulating latent conflict, it can prevent that conflict, and the consequent anger, being buried and turning into depression, lethargy and pessimism.

The espousal of dialogue as a methodological model is more than an ideological fad. A central problem facing complex organisations is bureaucratic inertia, the problem of how the sensitivity of a complex organisation to its, equally complex, environment can be maximised. The simple answer is, of course, 'information'. But the problem confronting organisations is that having acquired information they must use it intelligently. There are many recent examples of perfectly good information thrown up by research and information systems being wasted because there was no procedure to ensure its intelligent application. Most research and information systems produce WHAT-style information about a problem experienced by managers which is often rapidly translated into HOW-type responses, or solutions. What gets lost is the intervening WHY-process which endeavours to define the meaning of WHAT-style information in order to develop a more intelligent HOW-type response. The WHY-process is the dialogue, the pursuit of the answer, between those who are party to the problem.

The answer to the question of how can the sensitivity of a complex organisation to its, equally complex, environment be maximised is the WHY-process. The WHY-process, some of the products of which are recorded here is a robust and productive dialogue between parties with divergent interests. Collaborative research creates space for, and legitimises, a dialogue which is usually absent in hierarchical organisations. To this extent, collaborative research makes conscious use of the 'Hawthorn effect'. The Hawthorn effect describes the process in which people who discover that they are the subjects of research respond to this discovery by acting differently. While the Hawthorn effect can wreck conventional research it works to the advantage of the type of work reported here because change is the whole purpose of the research. The medium is also the method. In Chapter 9 of this book Chris Gostick, himself a director of social services, reflects on the contribution of such collaborative research to organisational change.

Research, dialogue and policy

The findings of the research and the recommendations of the standing conference will, in due course, be presented to the social services committee in the authority where the work was undertaken. If the recommendations are adopted they will be translated into council policy. If this happens the protracted and extensive dialogue developed through the standing conference will at last connect with the political dialogue in the local authority and, perhaps, we will witness the emergence of a very unusual sort of policy which both reflects and responds to the needs and concerns of young people in crisis, their foster parents and social workers and those who manage them.

This chapter has attempted to convey something of the approach adopted by the standing conference. Subsequent chapters will deal with its findings and their implications for practice and policy in greater detail. While it seems to us that the minimalist approach to disadvantaged young people has very serious shortcomings, we have no wish to engage in theoretical inversion by advocating a reversion to 'welfarism'. We argue instead for an optimal, 'ism-free' intervention characterised by a sensitivity to the rights, and a responsiveness to the rapidly changing needs, of young people in crisis.

References

Becker, H 1967 Whose side are we on? *Social Problems* **14** (3): 239–47
Blagg H, Smith D 1989 *Crime Penal Policy and Social Work*. Longman
Booker C 1980 *The Seventies*. Penguin
Bright J, Petterson G 1984 *Safe Neighbourhoods*. NACRO
DHSS 1983 *Local Authority Circular 3 (83) The Intermediate Treatment Initiative*. HMSO
Herron J 1981 Philosophical basis for a new paradigm. In Reason P, Rowan J (eds) *Human Inquiry*. John Wiley
King M 1988 *Making social crime prevention work — the French experience*. NACRO
McCormack M, Janus D, Burgess A 1988 Runaway youths and sexual victimisation: gender differences in an adolescent runaway population. *Child Abuse and Neglect* **10** (3): 387–95
Mathiesen T 1974 *The Politics of Abolition*. Martin Robertson
Millham S et al. 1989 *Lost in Care*. Saxon House
Morgan P 1978 *Delinquent Fantasies*. Temple Smith
Morris A et al. 1980 *Justice for Children*. Macmillan
Moynihan D P 1969 *Maximum Feasible Misunderstanding*. Free Press, New York
NACRO Youth Activities Unit 1988 *The Golflinks Project*. NACRO

Pitts J 1988 *The Politics of Juvenile Crime*. Sage
Schur E 1974 *Radical Non-intervention*. Prentice Hall, New York
Skynner R 1971 The minimum sufficient network. *Social Work Today* August
Smith C, Farrant M, Marchant H 1972 *The Wincroft Youth Project*. Tavistock
Thorpe D et al. 1980 *Out of Care*. Allen and Unwin
Young J 1986 The failure of criminology: the need for a radical realisim. In Matthews R, Young J *Confronting Crime*. Sage

2 Creating choices. Working with long-term solvent abusers

John Kilfeather and Viv Parker

This chapter gives an account of the development of a 'client-led' service with a group of young people who were engaged in solvent abuse. Despite their obvious and pressing problems none of the existing educational, recreational and welfare services had a clear responsibility for them. The chapter describes how, on the one hand, workers were able to redefine problems and mediate between the young people and these agencies, while on the other hand they supported them to make important choices about their lives.

Initial contact

In August 1985 John Kilfeather, one of the workers at the Chopin Intermediate Treatment Project, became aware of a group of young people who were publicly abusing solvents. They congregated on the southern end of the Chopin estate from early morning until workers left the Project building in the evening. Everybody who worked in the Project expressed concern about these young people, who seemed to be living chaotic lives. The group consisted of white males aged between 16 and 23 years. They looked gaunt and rough.

There had been a long history of solvent abuse on the Chopin estate. The local newspaper reported upwards of 100 children sniffing solvents on the estate. At a team meeting in November the staff discussed their concerns about these young people. They suspected them of being involved in a number of break-ins and attacks on the building. It was decided that John should spend some time in a 'detached' capacity in order to make contact, and negotiate the possible use of project facilities with the group.

Dave, a chronic abuser who was the first group member with whom John established contact, initially responded with mistrust

15

but eventually revealed that he sniffed solvents every day, even Christmas Day, as he had nothing else to do. He said that boredom was his main reason for abusing solvents. Having established a rapport with John, Dave told his friends that there was somebody in the Project who was willing to talk to them. During this initial stage Dave acted as mediator between the group and the project.

At this stage John raised the possibility of offering a service with other project staff. This created anxiety for them and some staff questioned whether the project had the resources, in terms of skills and time, to meet the needs of solvent abusers. Two major issues for staff were that these young people had a reputation for being disruptive and difficult to manage and that the additional work would impinge on the other services being provided. After discussing these issues, the team agreed that John should undertake a short-term piece of work, while the project leader would provide supervision for John. The group would be offered a one-and-a-half hour session once a week for six weeks, during which they would be introduced to photography and have use of the pool table.

John's main objective was to encourage these vulnerable young people to use the Project's resources. His intention was not to take a rehabilitative role with the solvent abusers and he made it clear during his conversations with Dave that his objective was not to stop them sniffing glue. One of the aims, however, was to assess their vulnerability and to ascertain whether they would be open to a rehabilitative form of work, with a longer-term aim of referral to a specialist agency.

The following proposal was agreed by the Project staff:

> It is proposed to engage the group in recreational and educational activities. The activity-based work will be used as a medium to promote further work with certain individuals within the group. This work will be in the areas of employment, housing and training. Issues around solvent abuse will be tackled on an individual basis alongside the work. If possible groupwork on solvent abuse will take place in the long term under the heading of 'Social and Health Education'.

Although membership varied the group was in fact made-up of 12 young men. Some group members wanted just to play pool but others were interested in photography. The three people who were interested in photography appeared intermittently over the six week period and appeared to gain a lot from it.

The pictures they produced were of a good quality and they were clearly overawed that they had access to these resources. The pool players had a similar attitude. Usually they would have to pay between 30p and 50p for a game, whereas the pool sessions were free in the Project. Over the six week period about five or six people turned up regularly. Their attitude and response was that of children much younger than their age and they seemed to thoroughly enjoy their contact with the Project.

Through informal discussions around the pool table and over cups of tea people slowly began to reveal aspects of themselves and their problems. Most of them had been using solvents for between six and seven years. They identified strongly with glue sniffing. They seemed on the one hand to be proud of it, while on the other they envied the people they knew who had stopped, or got married or had just moved out of the area. They mentioned being placed in boarding schools, being taken into care, violence at home, and the death of a friend who fell from a flat during a glue sniffing session. The stigma they now faced as adult glue sniffers and their fears for the future contrasted with the good times they had had as children, sniffing in the local playground. Then, glue gave them much more enjoyment, but now they experienced a more diluted form of the sensation. This was attributed to the body's changing tolerance of solvents.

Information obtained during sessions was relayed in supervision with the Project Leader and discussion took place at team meetings. During the six week period it became obvious that the group felt increasingly at ease in the Project. They began to volunteer information about their use of glue, the history of solvent abuse on the estate and their own friendship networks. Significantly, they were outside of all local facilities and had no contact with other agencies, with the exception of the police.

Many had problems related to housing. Two or three of them were homeless and were squatting in local flats, sleeping in the lift shafts or behind the Project. They were all long-term unemployed with little motivation to work. All had been involved in petty crime, mainly linked to obtaining money for solvents or stealing solvents from DIY shops. It became evident that some of the group members were not eating properly while others were receiving support from family and friends. It is a remarkable fact that John had come into contact with genuinely hungry people who were living in their own neighbourhood with no money and nowhere to live. On the basis of this information, the Project considered future work with the group and decided to extend it indefinitely. Over the next few months John often worked on his own with the group but other workers supported him by being in the building during group sessions in case anything went wrong.

Pen pictures of some of the group members

During this period, between four and ten people had attended the weekly group session of whom seven became the core group:

Dave
Dave was 20 years old, a thin man of medium height. He had a skinhead haircut and often had blisters around his lips. He was a chronic solvent abuser but presented as a small, vulnerable child. He appeared lonely and shy. He made little eye contact and he was usually acutely embarrassed when a woman spoke to him. He had a lovely smile.

Gordon
Gordon was 22, a tall, gaunt man whose clothes were usually stained with glue. His jacket pocket was always bulging with his tin of glue. When the group started Gordon was in prison, but he knew many of the people attending. On his release he remained on the periphery for about three months, literally standing outside the Project building, but refusing to come inside. Gordon's behaviour was unpredictable. At times he was easy going, but he could also be intimidating and was potentially violent. His attitude towards his addiction was very pessimistic. He believed that it was impossible for him to stop sniffing unless he was in prison.

Jack
Jack was 22 and presented a tough, macho image. Compared to the others he was well-dressed and had a strong work ethic. At this time he was squatting and suffering from a cut ligament in his hand. This was a self-inflicted wound following the ending of a relationship. He was sensitive and used glue in private to escape his feelings. He would deny that he had any problems and would be embarrassed if caught sniffing glue. Jack could be extremely likeable and helpful but under the influence of glue was short-tempered, aggressive and unreasonable.

Jimmy
Jimmy was 21 and lived with his parents. His appearance would vary according to his state of mind. He had severe bouts of glue-sniffing which often resulted in violence against property and people. However, he had a wide range of hobbies and could be interesting company when not intoxicated.

Peter
Peter was 19 years old, tall and lanky, and he identified himself as a 'mod'. He was a chronic solvent abuser and usually had red marks around his lips. He could be reckless and noisy when intoxicated with glue but the others regarded him as a 'comedian'. He had few social skills but a fairly open nature and was usually easy-going when sober.

Sam
Sam was 19 and lived with his mother. He was very thin and his physical health was poor. His appearance varied from well-dressed and image-conscious to the other extreme, when he wore old, worn-out clothes and did not change or wash. Sam was artistic with much unrealised talent. His misuse of glue was related to his emotional state. He could be extremely articulate and had insight into his situation. At other times he would be depressed and suicidal. Sam saw himself as being different from the others but still part of the group.

Tom
Tom was 23, a pleasant easy-going person but he could be violent when provoked. Tom had a stable relationship and presented as someone who had overcome his solvent abuse problems. He was not a regular attender but saw himself as a helper since he no longer used glue.

By March group members were turning up for the sessions on time and keen to get to the pool table. A hot meal, which they very much appreciated, was produced half way through every session. After the initial six weeks, only one person continued to maintain a strong interest in photography. This, together with the staffing problems at the Project, meant that the group sessions now focussed mainly on the provision of food and playing pool.

Since Jimmy was unable to pursue the interest in photography he had developed at the Project, John suggested he enrol at the local Adult Education Centre. Jimmy lacked the confidence to go on his own so John enrolled as well and they both completed a City and Guilds Certificate course. This way of working was unusual for John but he hoped it would give Jimmy an opportunity to break away from the other group members. By working with Jimmy in this way he was trying to loosen group influence so that he could become more independent. Unfortunately this did not happen.

First residential trip
John had contacted a Farm Trust which agreed to the group using its facilities in Somerset. The Trust is a registered charity set up by local people to provide an experience of rural and farming life for the residents of the borough. The residential trip took place in June.

Introducing the possibility of a residential break in Somerset took the group by surprise. Their immediate reaction was, would they have to stop glue sniffing? Would they need money? Could they trust John? Was this some kind of con? Could they trust one another to abide by any rules? They placed all the responsibility for the residential break on John, showing little commitment. Over the next few months John worked to get the group to accept some responsibility for planning, and setting goals and rules for the trip.

By this time the group had increased its membership from five to seven. There was obviously a network of glue sniffers in and around the estate and the existence of this group was attracting them to the Project. The glue sniffing bouts depended on whether members had received their unemployment benefit and whether they were depressed, happy or feeling indifferent.

The planning meetings were a way of promoting discussion about solvent abuse. Initially the group were reluctant to talk about it and they assumed that John, as a worker, was going to lay down the rules. He reversed that role and left it to them to create their own rules. They were adamant that it would be unfair to sniff solvents while they were away on holiday. They accepted the fact that they would be using another project's premises and there would be an issue regarding the reputation of the Farm Trust in Somerset. The rules they agreed regarding solvent abuse were that if any member of the group indulged in solvents during the residential break they should be sent back to London by train. This was a democratic decision made by the group.

During the planning sessions two people from the National Campaign Against Solvent Abuse visited the Project. John negotiated this visit with the group about three weeks in advance. The workers from the National Campaign met with the group and discussed the addictive qualities of solvents. The group were keen to carry on the sessions with the National Campaign, who agreed to come to the residential Trust one afternoon and bring someone who had been addicted to solvents and had managed to overcome his addiction.

Only four members of the group would commit themselves to the residential break; the others felt they would be unable to spend a week away without solvents. Although disappointed that four refused to go, John saw this admission of their inability to abstain from glue for a week as a positive statement to the staff. This allowed John to concentrate his efforts more fully on those people who were keen to go. The group members' concept of the residential break was that it was to be a visit to a 'health farm'. It took some time to convince them that they would not be committing themselves to an institution of that nature.

During the planning sessions, the group members started to speak more freely about their drug experiences and continued to do so whilst they were away from London. They talked about experiencing hallucinations of immense beauty and others which they found extremely frightening. Feelings of euphoria and elation were common to the group during the early stages of solvent abuse. It became evident that all of them were disaffected with their lifestyle because their dependence on solvents was socially and economically disabling.

Both staff and group members had no way of knowing what kind of withdrawal a long-term solvent abuser would experience during a week without solvents. Irrational emotional outbursts were common, although quickly dealt with. During the week away it became apparent that the group were sniffing solvents. When confronted they initially denied it. When they finally admitted it they experienced guilt, remorse and expressed concern that they had let the workers down. They said they secretly sniffed solvents late at night to avert their impending withdrawal. They used the drug so as not to affect their day-to-day programme.

In retrospect it appeared that the 'democratic' decision made by the group that anyone who used solvents should be sent home, was made with the best of intentions to meet, what they assumed to be, staff expectations. In reality, they were addicted to glue and unable to abstain from using it.

The relationships between group members were not conducive to staying off solvents. Their skills of evasion and their dependence on one another for support in their solvent abuse were complex. In general the residential break was a success and a valuable experience for everyone.

The group came to the residential break with little or no money, therefore they were dependent on the staff for food, activities and entertainment. The group's relationship with workers was strengthened because the day-to-day activities and the work programme enabled a dialogue to take place. The change of environment made a significant difference and meeting and talking with local people, and going for walks in the countryside, were conducive to reflection on their own life-styles. Significantly three of the group immediately got casual jobs on returning to London.

The journey back was difficult. Many of the group felt depressed and did not relish the thought of returning to London. The experience in Somerset had brought everyone closer together; feelings of nurture, security and enjoyment, the holiday environment, all seemed so distant as the reality of returning to London became imminent. Once back in London the group spoke excitedly of the holiday and impressed upon those who did not go that, if ever they had the opportunity to go away, they should do so.

July to December

When the group started again after a three-week break the idea of rehabilitation was introduced. The residential break had shown that a number of people were disaffected with their life-style and had expressed a desire to give up solvents and John wanted to capitalise on this. He visited various hostels and drug rehabilitation programmes and began to discuss with the group what rehabilitation units were available to them. Peter was the first person to show much interest in rehabilitation. He was considered to be an appropriate 'candidate' for rehabilitation for this although his chances were complicated by the fact that his brother was also a solvent abuser and another solvent abuser was living with them as a lodger. Peter was perhaps more open than other members to considering giving up glue. When he started to show interest in rehabilitation, he was mainly motivated by a desire to get away from the area. However, like many of the others, he was unrealistic about how easy rehabilitation would be. He thought that by simply leaving the local area his problems would be solved.

This reflected a progressive move on John's part to engage with the problem of the group members' dependency on solvents. From an impartial, non-interventionist position at the beginning of the group, he gradually began to be able to use his position of trust with group members to confront their solvent abuse in a way that would not have been possible earlier.

This period saw an increase in individual work with group members who dropped into the Project to see John. Sometimes this was for practical assistance with benefits but it was also for support in trying to give up solvents, or cope with bouts of depression which often led to a more intensive use of glue. As the Christmas period approached, many group members, having no money and no family ties, became very depressed. Some of them appeared with glue all over their clothes, they had blisters around their lips and showed considerable weight loss. This was a period of regression since prior to, and some time after, the residential break they had all kept themselves looking quite good.

Changes in the group

By December a co-worker for the group had been agreed. Viv started in January. It was not easy for her to enter a well-established group but the group members were on the whole friendly and welcoming. In the first few weeks group members tried to behave in ways which would not 'frighten' Viv away. They would, for example, check one another's swearing.

Controlling the use of glue

All the group members were addicted to glue. The degree of dependency varied between individuals yet their degree of dependency related to their current personal situation. There was no clearly discernible pattern.

Because they were all dependent on glue, any discussion about controlling use was threatening to them. Paradoxically the more the group talked about wanting to give up glue, the more solvents they used. Workers had to find a way of overcoming this. It was not easy and they tried a variety of methods; what succeeded one week could fail the next. There was no obvious answer.

One idea was that group members should hand in their tin of glue at the beginning of the evening meeting. This would work for some group members for a number of weeks and then they would refuse to do so. Another method was never to leave anyone alone in a room, because although they were not using solvents openly in front of the workers, whenever they were left alone they were tempted. This was very difficult to implement because there could be up to ten people in a building which has many rooms and was staffed by only two workers.

Beyond this, workers were not prepared to follow group members into the toilets, where a number of them would congregate to sniff glue. The possibility of not allowing group members in unless they handed in their tin was discussed. This was impossible to carry out, because unless staff were prepared to body search members there was no way of knowing whether they had a glue bag and so this strategy depended on individual honesty. Sometimes this worked, and glue bag and tins were handed in, but at other times it failed.

Another suggestion was that members leave the building for short periods in order to use glue outside. The point of this was to help individuals develop self control over their misuse of glue. Through helping them to abstain for two hours per week workers hoped to reinforce the fact that abstention was possible. Another reason for this approach was that workers wanted to avoid colluding with the group members. If they had openly permitted glue sniffing in the Project building it would have undermined the basic aim of the group. While it must be said that the clandestine use of glue often took place in the Project, the workers nonetheless attempted to retain the building as a kind of glue-free 'oasis'.

The workers' attempts at controlling the use of glue met with varying degrees of success. Workers consistently discouraged members' use of glue, and when they saw anyone sniffing they told them to stop. The aim was to give members a negative message when they used glue, and positive reinforcement when they went for periods of time without it.

The group members' high degree of dependency on solvents made them very pessimistic about the future. They felt hopeless and helpless. Workers tried to instill some feelings of hope for the future and a sense that they could be helped and could also help themselves.

Rehabilitation

The original aim of the workers was not rehabilitation. At the same time, this was an option which was available to those who were interested. Rehabilitation is the process whereby a person dependent on any drug first confronts and then starts to control his/her addiction. Beyond this, rehabilitation may also mean that a person is enabled to play a more active part in society by experiencing, so called, normal living and normal satisfactions.

To obtain more information on what rehabilitative possibilities were available John visited several drug dependency units, including a number of residential establishments working with drug addicts. He was surprised to find most of them did not regard solvent abusers as appropriate candidates for their establishments. They saw solvent abuse as specialist work. This differentiation probably reflects the fact that opiate abusers and solvent abusers tend to come from different class backgrounds. While hard drug users tend to come from a variety of class backgrounds, solvent abusers are invariably from low income working class homes and neighbourhoods. Solvent abusers seem to have more in common with the stereotype of a down-and-out alcoholic, as opposed to a hard-drug user. The culture and ethos of hard-drug users is very different from the habits of solvent abusers.

At about this time many group members were prepared to acknowledge they had a problem with glue, but most were very pessimistic about their chances of giving it up. Peter was the first to feel he might be able to succeed. The group members accepted that a change of life-style might act as a catalyst for other change in their lives. This could mean living in another locality, meeting new people with similar sorts of problems, or having contact with other helping and caring workers. This frightened them. Their dependency on solvents and on each other were both self-defeating. In many respects their relationships with one another were inhibiting their individual growth. The group's ethos was so strong that somehow they had lost their individuality. They needed individual space to grow, and find their own identity.

Workers did not develop a single model for bringing about change which would be appropriate for all group members. They tried instead a number of different approaches to rehabilitation. Peter had agreed to consider the Kaleidoscope Project as an alternative to his situation whilst others rejected this option at this stage. The Kaleidoscope Youth and Community Project based in Kingston, Surrey, is a hostel which offers an intensive residential rehabilitation programme to young adults who have suffered from drug abuse or mental illness. Peter was accepted by Kaleidoscope and funds were made available from Westminster Social Services under the Chronically Sick and Disabled Persons Act for the additional payments necessary for Peter's placement at the hostel. He moved into the hostel in May, about a year after that first residential trip.

Second residential trip

The second residential trip, in May, had a very different atmosphere from the previous one. This can be explained partly by the better attendance. Eight people attended this time, which created more potential for disagreement and left staff in a position of less control. During the planning process a more detailed programme for the residential break had been agreed, so everyone had a more realistic expectation of what was likely to happen. Last time the staff from the Farm Trust had anticipated that people would help out with some of the practical work at the Farm. This time there had been no explicit request in advance and people were free to help out if they chose to do so, but no one from the group showed interest.

The trip lasted for five days and every day there was a programme of activities. The day started with a group meeting, and when an incident occured the group met to discuss what the outcome should be. Although it is fair to say that this residential trip was successful, it was an exhausting experience for the staff. They were responsible for the group, and would stay awake with them until the early hours of the morning, and get up with them at the crack of dawn. As there were only two staff members, they took it in turn to ensure that one of them was available when a group member was awake. This tended to consolidate Viv's position in the group, since until then John had been seen as the person mainly in charge. Being aware of this the workers shared responsibilities, decision-making and the practical jobs. This contrasted with the previous occasion when, although John had been accompanied on the residential trip by another worker, their role was that of helper rather than co-worker.

The high degree of interdependence between the group members, and the way one person would be looked after when the group deemed it necessary was remarkable. For example, someone always made Gordon's breakfast in the morning. Gordon was not good at cooking and since his behaviour could be intimidating this was their way of accommodating his requirements. Spending so much time with them gave the workers the opportunity to talk to people on their own, to get to know them and make a better assessment of their needs.

One of the workers' aims for the residential trip had been to limit the use of glue. The use of glue was in fact higher than had been hoped. One of the reasons for this was that they were on holiday and they wanted a 'good time', and having a good time was associated with the greater use of glue. Since there were more people there was more glue available as there was always someone who had enough money to buy a tin. Generally they kept to the rules, but workers had difficulty controlling the use of glue in the building at night.

One day when Jimmy persisted in sniffing glue, the workers stopped the van and gave him a choice: either he stopped or he got out of the van. He would not stop, so eventually, with pressure from the others, he got out of the van. This created a dilemma for the group. Should they proceed with the activity, which was a day's outing, without Jimmy, or should they allow him to break the agreement? After some discussion and hesitation, the group decided to go back for Jimmy. He was relieved that they had returned for him and he continued on the outing without using glue in the van.

Interestingly, one of the things disclosed through the closeness generated by the residential trip was the paradox that although most of them were very keen to have relationships with women, some group members would, from time to time, have sexual liaisons with each other. This was an extremely sensitive area and one which they had great difficulty talking about. The extent of the social isolation eventually experienced by the chronic solvent abuser is apparent here. It becomes difficult to establish relationships, and so the abusers turn back and inwards to the peer group as a place of final acceptance. This powerful dynamic again endorses the strength of the abusing cycle and 'locks' the abuser even more strongly into the 'glue culture'.

In order to accommodate Gordon, another of the group members, the workers had to acknowledge that he was unable to go for long van journeys of more than an hour without using glue. For whatever reasons he found this intolerable, so an agreement was reached that there would be an hourly 'breather' when people could get out of the van. This proved successful and Gordon was able to comply with the agreement.

The return to London was the occasion on which it proved hardest to enforce this agreement. Everyone became extremely depressed, and once they became depressed they wanted to use glue to block off their feelings. The main reasons so many people came on the trip was that they had problems of housing or in their relationships, which meant that the level of depression within the group was high. This in turn led to greater use of solvents and consequently people had less control over their own behaviour.

One of the aims of the residential trip had been for each person to try a new activity: horse-riding, visiting some caves, outings to local social centres, a day at the coast, midnight walks and socialising with some of the local young people. Workers became aware that the level of social skills of some group members was extremely low, and that they operated on a 14–15 year old level, particularly when relating to women. When some of the lads met some local women it became apparent that they were sexually inexperienced and lacked basic knowledge. In the close atmosphere which had developed workers were able to offer advice, which they accepted.

On a day-to-day basis, group members co-operated with the shopping, cooking and washing up, although certain members helped more than others. In fact on the day they left some people put a lot of effort into tidying up the building.

Vast quantities of food were eaten during these five days. Most of the members were underweight and they took advantage of the opportunity to have good regular meals. By the end some of them were boasting about the weight they had gained.

One major concern during the residential trip was the question of violence. The degree of violence which took place was unacceptable to the workers. Jack was woken by Sam, who was demanding some glue in the early hours. Jack was incensed at being woken and hit Sam, who reacted by dashing downstairs to get a knife. The workers were woken by the commotion and intervened. Sam had the knife in his hand and was intent on using it. He became even more enraged when the workers blocked his way. It took a lot of careful handling to de-escalate the situation which was, by then, extremely tense and potentially dangerous. Following this incident the workers considered returning to London. In the morning they presented their concerns to the group. It was only when group members reassured them that it would not happen again and that they would take extra responsibility that it was decided to remain in Somerset.

The workers attempted not to undermine the group's responsibility or react to their extreme behaviour by taking over the decision-making. They aimed to work with the group to change unacceptable behaviour by helping them find solutions.

A positive outcome of the second residential trip was that the group now accepted that having regular meetings was the way to make decisions. As a result meetings were more constructive and better organised with a higher level of co-operation and participation.

Weekly group sessions

Because the activities during the residential trip were so successful the workers decided to implement a timetable of activities at the Project. When the time for an outing came along, however, some group members resisted it fairly strongly. This was attributed to a lack of confidence and low self-esteem, although ironically it emerged that the skills that group members did possess had been acquired at boarding schools and Youth Custody Centres.

In October the decision was taken to keep the group running until the following March and this was presented to the group. The workers reiterated that the purpose of the group was to make people aware of their options in relation to their life-style and to help them to control their habitual solvent abuse.

Individual work

Partly as a result of the recognition that the group was inhibiting the development of individual members, the workers started to offer people more structured individual sessions at the Project. Following the residential trip the workers became increasingly aware of peoples' personal situations and sometimes the only way to help was to see them on their own. They knew that when a group member went through a crisis they would come to the Project and expect to be seen and receive assistance. Workers found that one way of trying to control demands on their time was to offer the young men a regular slot in the week when staff would be available. Group members tended to see these sessions as a helpful way of reinforcing their own individual identity, since they received some attention on a one-to-one basis.

A wide variety of issues were discussed during these individual sessions which included housing, rehabilitation, control of solvent abuse, personal relationships, DHSS problems, confrontations with the police, problems relating to parents and employment.

Additional contact with the group

During this period the group was fairly dependent on the workers. They regularly stood around outside the building waiting for them. The workers tried to control this as much as possible but at the same time respond in a positive way. Following the residential trip, for example, a number of group members wanted another holiday. The workers helped four of them to go away on their own by providing tents and sleeping bags and by helping them to plan and organise the trip. It turned out to be an enjoyable holiday for them and another milestone in their path to recovering self-esteem.

Preparation for ending

In January, two years on from the group's first beginnings, the workers began to prepare the group for its closure. This was a difficult decision, but in the view of the workers a necessary one. When the group had started, strategies were employed to improve the quality of each person's life and to increase their self-esteem. This had, to some extent at least, been achieved and members had also developed self-awareness about their problems. It seemed clear, however, that the solutions to these problems could not be found within the group. The group had now 'graduated' from a dependence on one another towards greater independence, and it seemed to the workers that to continue the group might serve to inhibit individual growth.

For example two young men living in a rehabilitative hostel continued to attend the group but they also continued to maintain their relationship with the group outside the Project. The main reason for their return was to maintain their position within their peer group network and this meant that, while at their hostel they did not indulge in solvent abuse, on their return to the estate they would sniff glue with their friends.

As long as everyone was a member of the group they felt a strong loyalty to one another. Even though an individual might try to restrict or reduce their use of glue, the others would encourage them to participate in glue sniffing sessions, even if it meant sharing their glue around. People were unable to develop their own personal interests as the group undermined anyone who tried to break away. They were also extremely competitive, not only for their status within the group but also for the attention of the workers. In symbolic terms one might say that the workers were identified in a parental role and the Project was viewed as '*home*'. The Project offered security, comfort and warmth. It attempted to meet some of their basic needs and when they had no one else to turn to they knew that the workers would always try to help. However, the group sessions seemed to be preventing the maturation process of leaving home and moving towards independence which normally takes place during adolescence. So, the workers explained that the group was ending but that the individual work would continue. The offer of individual sessions was seen as a means of ending the group without rejecting the members.

There was a marked progress during this period with certain individuals, while others fell into bouts of chronic solvent abuse. The workers felt concerned for them and encouraged them to participate in individual sessions.

The final session

The final session went remarkably well. Everyone was on their best behaviour although the workers were initially suspicious at the odd way group members were behaving. It later emerged that this was because they had pooled their money in order to buy a small gift and a card for the workers. The meal was drawn out because people took the opportunity to sit and talk about the life of the group. Everyone was able to share positive memories but at the same time acknowledge their sadness about the ending. People said 'Hasn't the two years gone quickly?' and recalled how the group had first started and how much they had changed since then. John was able to tell the group that he had observed a lot of positive changes over the time since they had all first met. Viv shared how proud she had felt about being asked to join the group once it had been established. Group members commented on what they had got from the group. For this final session, glue was not an issue and no one sniffed it inside the building. Most participants identified the fact that they were using less glue now than they were two years ago, and this was reflected in their state of physical well-being. At the end of the session everyone left in a very adult way. They said goodbye, thanked the workers for everything and left the building. The workers were relieved and pleasantly surprised that everything had gone so smoothly.

Postscript

Following the ending of the group in March, most members took up the offer of individual counselling and have continued to receive it since.

Evaluating the group

To evaluate any piece of work is not an easy task. It would be naive to imagine that there is only one formula or one approach. The evaluation would be incomplete if it concentrated on the groupwork process or on the individual's development within the group. At the same time, one is aware that for each person, the group was only a small part of their total life experiences. Yet it appears that the importance and influence of the group was far greater than one might have anticipated in view of the number of hours members spent in contact with workers. This is significant, and perhaps indicates the potential for 'low profile' work with peer groups of solvent abusers as an alternative to the more intensive approach adopted by many rehabilitation programmes. Another attraction of this approach is the tendency not to frighten the abuser off and to engage him at an earlier point than the collapse that so often precedes admission to intensive programmes.

Before the group ended members were interviewed about their experience of it. When asked in what way the group had helped

Creating choices 31

them, and if they had changed in any way over the two year period, one person replied: 'I think the group has done a lot for me; it meant something to look forward to. Sometimes I couldn't wait for Tuesday nights'. Another person said: 'It has shown me ways of stopping sniffing'. Another stated: 'The group has helped me to relate to my problems, made me more aware, and I am able to communicate better and put my points across'. Another stated that: 'It was the most major thing to happen over the last two years'.

Everyone in the group said that group meetings were a good way of making decisions but at the same time admitted it was a difficult process and the least enjoyable part of the Tuesday evening sessions.

The main reasons, they said, were that there was always somebody messing around during the meetings because they felt depressed or because they did not feel particularly co-operative. When asked if John and Viv had influenced the group members in any way, they said: 'Yes. I've been able to talk to them like my Mum and Dad. They will understand'. Another person said: 'They've helped educate me to think'. Everyone in the group acknowledged that John and Viv had become important to them and had influenced them in one way or another.

Management involvement

The Solvent Abuse Group was unusual. The difficulties of the members were the responsibility of a variety of agencies and sections of the social services department but none of these services saw it as their distinct task to address their problems. Arguably, few social services departments would have been prepared to support a new initiative which involved working with long-term solvent abusers, but the Chopin Project had the backing of management for this piece of groupwork despite the fact that strictly speaking it fell outside of an IT Project's brief, principally because the group members were all young adults.

During the course of the group an Inner City Initiatives on Drugs was launched. One result of this was that a special working party, a 'Drugs Task-Force', was established. This was fortuitous for the Solvent Abuse Group because it meant that not only was there wider interest but also money for work relating to drug abuse. These factors appear to have influenced the agency with the result that management was prepared to resource and support the running of the group. In addition, line managers showed a lot of interest in the way the group developed and the problems which arose from the ongoing work. The outcome was that the group was allowed to run for a total of two and a half years so that it could come to a natural conclusion without pressure being put on workers to end it prematurely.

Attendance

Attendance is a criterion which is often used for evaluation purposes. While it has limited usefulness it does indicate in a very general way whether the group was meeting some of the members' needs. During the first two phases no detailed records were kept but generally attendance was high. Later a weekly form was completed after each evening group session. It appears that seven people attended most sessions and sometimes there were eleven. In the final year there was a core group of eight, and occasionally other people, who were, or had been solvent abusers, would participate in the group sessions. On the basis that 80 per cent of the time seven members attended each group session, we can say attendance was unusually high for this type of group.

Physical health

During discussions with members of the group, physical health became an issue. The workers felt that members should be aware of information about the long-term effects of solvent abuse. Few members could identify the physical effects of long-term abuse and when they did it would usually follow a glue-sniffing binge over a period of two or three days. They would complain of headaches, backaches, and pains in the chest. One member aggravated an existing medical condition and subsequently suffered from collapsed lungs after a glue-sniffing binge. However, the majority of group members did not appear to suffer any long-term physical effects from abuse. Prolonged and continued solvent abuse did affect members' appetites, and most of them were underweight. The weekly group sessions always included a meal and the health of some individuals who had not been eating properly improved as a result. During residential breaks, vast quantities of food were consumed, and individuals would comment at the end of the week about how much weight they had put on.

During periods when group members were homeless, they would be allowed into the Project at times outside the normal sessions. They could then get hot food, tea and warmth. This helped them survive the cold winter months. Meeting for sessions at a specific time each week helped to create a structure in their otherwise chaotic lives and workers observed that members' mental and physical health were interrelated. If they were eating properly and their social situation was reasonably organised they would start looking better and feeling better, and, as a result, their self-esteem would increase. The workers would reinforce any improvement and try to convey to them the connection between chronic solvent abuse and physical and mental ill-health.

Change can be observed by comparing the difference between Christmas the first year and the following Christmas. The first Christmas was a more frustrating and depressing time for group members. There was chaotic and persistant abuse of solvents, marked ill-health and weight loss. A year later, Christmas was a more normal, festive occasion with a general improvement in members' health and a reduced level of solvent abuse.

Over the two years there were several occasions when individuals made suicide attempts. None was so serious that it led to a hospital admission, but first aid had to be administered. They would talk about their depression and how they were contemplating suicide. If the workers knew of this, they were able to offer extra support until the depression passed. During the life of the group none of the members died. This is significant since prior to the group some of their friends had died through the 'indirect' effects of solvent abuse.

Although there was an improvement in group members' physical and mental health, they remained vulnerable. When an individual encountered any sort of problem, this affected them emotionally and they would quickly regress. For example, when Jack's relationship with his girlfriend finished, he went on a solvent binge. However, these relapses would only be temporary.

Offending

Most of the group members have a long history of petty offending, 80 per cent of them had spent some time in custody. During the two years, only two of them were involved in any further offending. This was different from what had happened prior to the formation of the group. One person was involved in a fight and went to court; another, during a period of homelessness, was arrested by the police for behaviour likely to cause a breach of the peace. Another person, who had started to attend the group in the early days but never became a core group member, continued to re-offend and spent a considerable period of time in custody. It seemed that membership of the Solvent Abuse Group was one reason for individuals changing their behaviour. People looked forward to the weekly session and did not want to miss any of them. They therefore had an additional incentive to stop committing offences and remain in the community.

Housing

Housing and solvent abuse seem to be closely interrelated, with one factor invariably affecting the other. When people were homeless or had poor housing they used more solvents in order to block out their problems. On the other hand, because neighbours were not prepared to put up with the behaviour which resulted from solvent abuse, members were liable to eviction.

About four group members became homeless during the life of the group. At one stage, it seemed that one possible solution would be to acquire a house that would accommodate all of the members who needed housing and which would be staffed by workers from social services. Although this would have solved their immediate problems it would have been counter-productive in the long term. Each person needed a different solution because they had different needs.

The cost of the hostel places for the group members who were referred to Kaleidoscope Youth and Community Centre was paid by the social services department. Another two people were accommodated under the Homeless Persons Act on the basis that they were vulnerable due to their solvent abuse. They were subsequently housed in permanent accommodation, one by the housing department and another by a housing association. They remain within the borough but are not living on the Chopin Estate.

A fifth person became homeless together with his girlfriend, who was pregnant. He was eventually rehoused by a housing association. A sixth has discussed with us the possibility of moving from his present accommodation which is very close to the estate. Discussions continue on whether he should go to some sort of independent living project or to a hostel. As a result of involvement with the group the housing situation of the majority of group members has improved considerably.

Changes in attitude and behaviour

Over the life of the group most of the members developed strong relationships with the workers. This meant that they became dependent and put a lot of trust in them. The workers were able to use this relationship to help them identify some of their own weaknesses and strengths. As a result there were changes in their attitudes and behaviour and a move towards independence.

Over the period members became more honest in their relationships with the workers. In the early days there had been occasions when items had been stolen from the Project but this ceased. Members became far more polite to other workers in the Project and appeared less desperate. They now had somewhere and someone to whom they could take their anxieties and the workers encouraged them to do this.

There were obvious changes in the way members related to women. Although workers were concerned about their violent behaviour both towards each other and other people, they were more prepared to talk about what was acceptable and what was not acceptable. On occasions when their behaviour had not been acceptable in the Project, they would acknowledge this and apologise — something which they had been unable to do earlier on in the life of the group.

Overall the group learnt to bring difficulties with which they were unable to cope to the workers, who in return were able to give them advice or support. As a result members developed their social skills, and became far more competent in dealing with outside agencies, like the DHSS and housing departments, without becoming verbally aggressive. This in turn meant they became more confident and had higher self-esteem.

By the time the group ended, all the members had changed some of their behaviour which now appeared more age-appropriate and mature.

Use of glue

One of the main aims of the group became to try to motivate the members to control their abuse of glue. Until the group ended, controlling the use of glue within the group sessions continued to be a problem.

The aim became not so much solely to make them stop using glue but rather to help them acknowledge that they had choices. Workers would on occasion feel a sense of failure when it was obvious that the group and individuals were over-indulging in the use of glue. The only way to continue working with them was to remember that the aim of the group was not just to make them stop. If that had been the aim, then the group had clearly failed. It aimed to help people acknowledge that glue-sniffing and its consequences were problems which, with help, they could tackle if they chose to do so.

Conclusion

In the aftermath of the group, the situation regarding solvent abuse was extremely positive. Although members continued to be friends, they no longer met on a regular basis. This allowed them to develop their own interests and identity. Peter and Dave, the two people at a rehabilitation hostel, no longer came to the estate on a regular basis. When they did, they would see one or two of their friends but not the whole group. They reduced their use of solvents drastically to a point where it was more within their control. Jimmy and Jack, who were rehoused outside the area, were far more settled and much less dependent on glue. Gordon, who set up his own household with his girlfriend and newly-born child, made a lot of use of the counselling sessions but continued to use large amounts of glue. Two other members kept in touch with the workers. Another stopped using glue completely for a number of months, but after a close relationship ended, went on a binge. One other person intermittently met up with one of the workers, but progress was slow.

The work described here was a journey without maps, an exploration rather than a prescription. There are many lessons to be learned from it but perhaps the two most important are that it was rooted in a commitment to accepting and valuing these young people and their view of the world and that it moved at their pace towards objectives they had defined for themselves.

3 Breaking the silence: developing work with abused young people in care

Lydia Ball, William Chatterton, Marie Clarke, Josephine Cullen, Rachael Hetherington, John Kane, Chris Iveson, Carol Knights, Heather Loxley, Maggie Phelan, Jill Roucroft and Robin Solomon Roychowdhury

This chapter examines the dilemmas for those providing services for abused young people in the care of the local authority and ways in which workers can be helped to work more effectively.

Introduction

The recent history of child protection has seen a series of major investigations each bringing with it a novel revelation about the dangers to children from abusing adults. Amongst these, events at Cleveland clearly illustrated the need to be aware that abuse is not restricted to particular strata of families, but is present across the whole social and economic spectrum. Accordingly social workers have approached investigations of abuse with a new sensitivity and a preparedness to consider the possibility of abuse in situations where this might well have been disregarded before — to 'think the unthinkable'.

Similarly, the 'discovery' of ritual abuse, focused around enquiries in Rochdale in 1990, has made practitioners more aware of the existence of organised groups of abusing adults. This has endorsed a need for practitioners to be vigilant where there is suspicion of 'networks' of abusers, and has made all the more important effective inter-agency co-operation surrounding the investigation of abuse.

More recently, a new piece has been added to the puzzle following prosecution of members of extended families living in Kent. This case has shown that some family groups routinely exchange their children for the sexual gratification of the adults. This abusing pattern emerges as one which is passed from one generation to another and accordingly reflects how profoundly abuse can become historically established within some families.

While these examples refer to instances where sexual abuse has been in the fore (and our own concerns in this chapter are with the survivors of all forms of abuse) the impact of these, and other, disturbing exposés on social services departments has, nevertheless, been to generate a strong pressure to improve child protection systems for *assessment* and *intervention*. Better communication between the relevant agencies is emphasised, as is a broad exchange of information beyond the previous parochial boundaries of each profession. In the light of current awareness of the extent and variety of child abuse, a new openmindedness is apparent, with the result that abuse is being recognised in situations when formerly it would not have been. In turn, a clearer recognition of abuse has led to better understanding of the action needed to protect children, and removal from the abusive situation can often be the emerging course of action. This has subsequently impacted on the care system in some authorities, since the evolution of child protection practice has been accompanied by increases in the number of wardship cases and a higher incidence of the admission of whole sibling groups into care.

It is at this point, those stages following reception into care, that this chapter takes up the problem. With the focus so strongly on assessment and intervention in child protection cases, we determined to review those services that abuse survivors who enter care receive from their new carers and to examine how provision could be improved to better provide for the sometimes quite damaged and disordered youngsters received into care after child abuse. When definitive action is taken and reception into care is adopted it is arguable that for many the problem is seen as stopping there. Another child protection scandal may have been averted, but as the sighs of relief die down the question is left: 'how will the needs of the youngsters now in care be met?' Providing appropriate care for damaged young people can be an expensive and time-consuming activity and there are indications that local authorities have yet to revise their care provision to a standard comparable with their, by now, significantly improved front-line child protection services. We set out to see if this assertion was true in the local authority under review.

Setting the scene

In the summer of 1989 members of staff in an inner-city local authority social services department (SSD) and two researchers from the West London Institute Department of Social Work set out to 'produce a discussion document and policy recommendations concerning the problems of abused young people in care' for presentation to the authority's social services committee.

The group consisted of:

Two field social workers from area teams
A residential social worker
A team leader from the community fostering section
A team leader from an IT centre
A team leader from an NHS-linked family therapy centre
A Child Protection Co-ordinator
The two researchers

We were given a very wide brief initially. The overall objective was to look at services for children in care who had been abused. The brief included looking at their 'systems careers' compared with other young people who had been abused but remained at home, while reviewing the decision-making process which led to reception into care and placement. For reasons which will become apparent, we focussed initially on identifying the target group and subsequently our work focussed on the resources available to these young people and at ways in which these could be developed.

The breadth of our original brief mirrored the breadth and complexity of the problem of abused young people in care. The work of the group concerned the attempt to define and come to terms with (one aspect of) this problem. The first task that we identified for ourselves was the relatively modest one of ascertaining the number of young people (aged 11+) who were in care and had been abused. We hoped to acquire general descriptive data about them, the resources used for them and their system careers. We planned to do this by unearthing the data held in the local authority's information systems and interviewing the children and their carers. We also hoped to collect information about resources available to abused young people in or out of care.

We based our consideration of abuse and neglect on the definitions given in the borough's child protection guidelines. We were aware, however, that these definitions are invariably open to widely varying, and ultimately subjective, interpretation.

Our findings are based on information from five sources. These were the statistical information held formally by the local authority, the replies to a questionnaire about individual children in care, the feedback and discussion at 'open forums' described elsewhere in the book, interviews with children and interviews with foster carers.

Local authority statistics

With regard to the number of abuse-survivors in care, the problem was that we had no idea whether we were talking about ten, or one hundred and ten children, and this was important because the scale and scope of further work depended on an answer to this question. The only figure available to us from the statistics was that 135 children aged 11+ were currently in care. While there was an age and gender breakdown, there was no indication of race, ethnicity or reason for admission into care. The information from the statistics about these children gave us the following information:

Placement	Per cent (Base 135)
In residential care	30
Fostered	47
Home on trial	10
Other	13
Legal status	
Voluntary care	64
All non-voluntary	36

As no information was held about reasons for entry into care, we made no further use of these figures except as a starting point. The statistics were disappointing as a useful data-base for research, but probably did not differ much from the elementary information collected in most local authorities.

Information from the questionnaires

We decided, therefore, that the most satisfactory way to collect the information we needed would be to go directly to the workers themselves. With that in mind we constructed a questionnaire, which was sent out to the field social workers of all young people (11+) notified to us by the statistical returns as being in care. We also sent this questionnaire to each of the youngsters' residential carers or foster carers.

Some of our responses to the questionnaire indicated that a number of the children about whom we had written to them were no longer in care. While we have no means of knowing whether any particular group of children were wrongly recorded as being in care, it would seem more likely that these were children in voluntary rather than statutory care. The actual replies to the questionnaires took a long time to come in and we received few from residential social workers and foster parents. However, we did have enough returns to go ahead with a 'modest' analysis.

Ultimately, 78 questionnaires were returned, giving information about 64 children. We estimated that this gave us information about approximately half of the young people in care. We had no way of knowing whether there was any particular bias in the return, but it is possible that there was a bias towards reporting about abused children, in that workers involved with children who they believed had been abused may have been more likely to complete the questionnaire, since it concerned these children. Most of the returns (50) were from field workers, 16 were from foster carers and 12 were from residential carers.

When we analysed the data from our questionnaire we noted that of the 64 young people about whom we had information, 24 were known to have been physically or sexually abused at the time they were received into care. In 37 cases abuse or neglect were among the reasons given for admission to care and 18 had disclosed previous physical or sexual abuse while in care. A further 6 were *thought* to have been abused before coming into care even though this was not known at the time and there had been no subsequent disclosure. Two children had been abused in the time that they were in care. In total, therefore, 46 of the 64 had definitely been abused. If we include neglect, the figure rises to 61. The realisation emerged, therefore, that in this local authority the likelihood that an adolescent entering care or still in care at 11+ *has not* been abused or neglected is slight.

Having found that so many young people in care had been abused, we wanted to know whether such abuse affected the choice of placement. Over half of the young people were placed in foster care and the rest were placed in the authority's own children's homes. Only three were in private and voluntary facilities and at that time none were in regional resource centres or secure units.

About one third of the young people in both foster care and residential care are known to have been abused at the time of placement. There is no evidence that known abused children were more likely to be placed in one or the other types of placement. The reasons why youngsters ended up where they did are manifold, with perhaps the major division between residential care and foster placement being determined on the one hand by availability and on the other by the young person's stated preference.

Table 3.1: Placement of young people known to be/not known to be abused on admission to care

	Abused	Not known to be abused	Total
Foster care	13	21	34
Residential assessment	2	2	4
Other residential	6	12	18
Other	3	5	8
Total	24	40	64

We explored the relationship between young peoples' legal status on admission to care and whether they were known to have been abused before entry into care. Table 3.2 illustrates these findings, which have important implications for the organisation of resources in the wake of the implementation of the 1989 Children Act, as will be discussed later.

Table 3.2: Legal status of abused young people

	Abused	Not abused	Total
Voluntary care	8	13	21
All non-voluntary:			
Care order	9	12	21
S. 3 Child Care Act 1980	3	6	9
Wardship	4	9	13
Total	24	40	64

Information from the open forums

The questionnaires were yielding information about the extent of the problem, but we also needed information about the responses of the people who were directly involved. One way we tackled this was to use the 'open forums' (special open meetings convened during the course of the research) to discuss initial findings and future work. At the first open forum we took a 'straw poll' amongst all those present (ranging from social work staff to the director) asking them to surmise how many young people of 11+ in care, had been abused, on the basis of their own professional experience. Most people thought that 70 per cent or more of these children had been abused. It is very interesting that this estimate supported so closely the information yielded by the questionnaires.

We also used the first open forum to present three hypothetical cases to workers and foster carers for discussion. The aim of these discussions was to see how far the decision-making process about reception into care was influenced by information about the behaviour or life history of a young person. Each of the three groups were given a different version of the same case. In all the versions the child was described as showing the same behaviour; in the first group there was no further information, the second group was also told that the child had been abused, while the third group was told that the child had been sexually abused. The groups were asked to devise a care plan for the child. We were interested to find that although the child's behaviour was described as the same in all cases, the care plans differed according to the historical information given. We were concerned about this, as our questionnaire data was suggesting that in reality an adolescent admitted to care with behavioural problems was very likely to have been physically and/or sexually abused.

While this was interesting it could not be considered 'hard' data. The information that came from these groups which had a greater impact on our thinking was something unplanned and unexpected. In the groups we had residential social workers, field social workers and foster carers. We quickly realised that residential carers and foster carers had never previously had an opportunity to meet. Clearly they felt a great interest in each others' experience. During the case discussions, it became clear that similar children with similar problems were being cared for in both settings and that there was nothing to choose (in the eyes of the carers) between the problems confronted by either group of workers. There also seemed to be a good measure of agreement that, whatever the formal structures might be, foster carers felt better supported than residential workers. It became apparent from these groups how similar were the needs and tasks of all carers for adolescents, yet the foster carers felt able to take on tasks which seemed 'impossible' to the residential workers. While they felt that this was partly because they were only dealing with one adolescent rather than a group (and that it was therefore easier to contain problems) it did not seem that the children they were dealing with were any less disturbed or unmanageable. This was not a reflection on the capabilities of the residential carers but a reflection of the system within which they were working.

Information from the foster carers

We felt that we should learn more from the foster carers about the work they were doing and, in particular, how they managed to cope with the high levels of stress involved in adolescent foster care. They described a very effective network of support. This was provided partly on an informal basis by foster carers for other foster carers, and partly by the link workers of the fostering section. The informal network depended in the first place on the work of the formal network to bring it into existence. The foster carers described having met other foster carers initially through the fostering support meetings and then having constructed, often on a geographical basis, their own system of informal links. Both the formal and the informal networks were sometimes called upon for practical help and relief, but what was most often found to be useful was the availability of consultation. The foster carers valued being able to talk a problem through with someone who was outside the situation but understood through their own experience, in preference to 'expert' advice or emergency intervention by social workers at points of crisis. The foster carers were indeed very experienced, and this raises the question of how typical their response might have been, but they had arrived at a way of working that enabled them to foster successfully some extremely demanding adolescents. What they had developed might be seen as a model to offer to less experienced workers. When they were asked for suggestions for improving the system, the foster carers were interested in extending the existing support system to include a 'hot line consultancy service' which could be telephoned at any time so that the carer could talk through what was happening in an emergency.

Information from the young people

Interviews with the young people on the receiving end of these services illustrate some fundamental principles about the needs of children and young people in care. The respondents were chosen at random from our questionnaires and were interviewed by students from a CQSW course. The students were told only the names, ages and ethnicity of their interviewees.

From the questionnaires, we selected a random group of 12 adolescents to be interviewed. For a variety of reasons we were unable to interview all of them. Some had left care during the project and did not wish to take part, some who were still in care also refused. The field social workers in some cases asked that the young person should not be approached.

The care experience of the young people varied from one who had been in care and with the same foster parents since the age of one, to another who had had five foster placements. Although the questionnaire covered wider ground, the comments young people made about their involvement in decision-making and being heard and supported were of particular interest. One 15 year old had had the same social worker for four years, all her time in care. Her relationship with this social worker was of very great importance to her; she was very clear about the means by which she could contact her social worker and how often she would see her; she felt that her social worker listened to her and she referred to work they had done together. Another child, who had

had several foster placements did not feel that she was listened to in deciding what would happen to her. She felt that placement decisions were taken by the social worker, and she sometimes did not know what was going on. She had a very clear view about what the task of the social worker *should* be; the social worker should look very carefully at a placement before placing someone, should make an assessment which included the views of the child concerned in the process, and should visit regularly. She did not feel that she had had this experience.

Any social worker who feels doubtful about whether their work is valued by adolescents could be reassured by these responses; the young people knew what help they needed and valued it when they got it. This work takes a great deal of time, so it is also helpful that the young people gave some indications of ways in which some tasks could be shared. One child talked about work he had done with his social worker in relation to his life story. He felt that this had been very difficult and had been taken too quickly, but appreciated now (several years later) that it had been useful; indeed he had found it useful to continue to find out about his past. He had however, at the time, got his foster carer to intervene to halt the process of this work, and his foster carer was the person he named as being the person who listened to him, and to whom he would go with problems. It raises the question whether his foster carers might not have been enabled to do the life story work with him themselves.

The use of specialist resources

One of the tasks that the research group set out to undertake was a review of the treatment and care facilities for abused adolescents in care. We quickly ran into problems. Simply to compile a list of agencies was obviously inadequate, while an accurate evaluation of the capacity of agencies to respond to the problem requires detailed records of use and outcome, which were non-existent. The group's researches demonstrated the scale and complexity of the task of holding and providing information on child care resources. This was a negative finding, in the sense that we were unable to make any coherent progress, but important in its implications for management systems. Consideration of resources inevitably therefore moved us to consider when and whether specialist resources were used for abused children and how non-specialist resources could be enabled to respond.

Thus the project team was uncovering another problem. Although the request for specialist services was increasing, the knowledge about what those specialist services actually offered was declining. The burgeoning of the private sector of childcare meant that much was on offer, but what exactly was being offered was unclear. People suspected that what was being offered was probably not very different from what they themselves were offering, but there was no way of verifying this. This further confused the debate about what was the best service to provide for the young people we were identifying. The more divergent the possible treatments, the more chaotic the experience for the service providers. It seemed a logical progression to re-examine the possibility of providing appropriate care within the structure already in place. If the exorbitant amounts spent on sending children out of the system to get specialist help could be rerouted back into the system to improve the services for all children, it would reflect more the reality which we were uncovering that *most* children in that system needed such specialist care. In the long term, by funneling money to the few, the majority were getting a second rate service, which meant less support for workers dealing with difficult young people. Ironically the result was that young peoples' difficulties were further exacerbated by shortfalls in care services and this increased the likelihood of them being ejected from the system into specialist services, while the remaining services ran down even further.

While the research was proceeding, the social worker from the family therapy centre initiated a programme of consultancy sessions with the staff group of a residential home for 10 young people. The work was based on brief solution-focused counselling developed at the Marlborough Family Centre (George, Iveson and Ratner 1990), and approaches developed in Australia at the Eastwood Family Centre (Durrant 1987) in work with sexually abused adolescents. The residential workers said they had gained support from these sessions which had focused their discussions and enabled them to identify positive and viable goals for their work. More significantly, they had noted a considerable improvement in young people who had been the focus of these sessions.

The implications for policy and practice

The information gained from our questionnaires and replicated in the open forum was not comprehensive, however, we feel it is reasonable to conclude that the majority of adolescents in care in this authority at this time had been abused (although this was often not known at the time they entered care). We also found nothing to suggest that the experience in this local authority was in any way distinctive or peculiar and this leads us to believe that were a similar exercise to be undertaken in other inner city authorities, the results would most likely be very similar.

It follows from this that all carers need to work with the reality that the child or young person for whom they care is more likely than not to have been abused. Because we do not know at the outset which children have been abused, and in some cases we may never know with any certainty, all care placements must aim to be 'good enough' for abused children. It cannot be a question of providing specialist services for the few; we have to provide a service for all young people in care which has the capability of responding to the needs of abused young people. In looking at services for abused adolescents we therefore felt that we had to look at the services for all adolescents in care. The most important services are the local authority residential and foster care services through which, at some point, all adolescents in care must pass.

The carers

How then could the carers of these children be enabled to provide the level of care that is needed without developing a service which, by acknowledging the likelihood of abuse, serves to stigmatise the survivors of abuse? The primary aim of all care is to provide a flexible and sensitive response to the needs of children and young people and, in the right circumstances, this can be achieved. People work best when they feel supported, have training which promotes their confidence, a network to turn to in times of stress and some ownership of the decisions they must implement. They also need a range of provision relevant to the needs of the care population.

For such provision to be achieved managers within the care system created access to reliable information about the numbers of children in care, their racial, cultural and religious affinities, something of their life history and current needs. The Children Act (1989) emphasises the importance of such information in planning for proper residential or foster care for adolescents.

There is also a need for systematic monitoring of the uses to which foster care and residential care are put. This would throw some light on the question of the extent to which placement is determined by availability rather than choice; and if it is choice, whose choice? It would also be possible to establish when and why private or voluntary residential homes are used. Without this information any evaluation of the effectiveness of different forms of care is impossible.

As we noted above, whereas foster parents felt that they had adequate opportunity for consultation, residential workers felt unsupported, indeed beleaguered, in their attempts to work effectively with abused young people. Research by Menzies (1970) about the organisation of hospitals demonstrated how young nursing staff defended themselves against the anxiety and pain of their patients by a process of distancing and denial. This was echoed in the hospital system and structure. A similar process may affect residential care workers faced with the pain and distress of abused young people, and, likewise the system and structure of children's residential establishments. This process of organisational defence may be inevitable unless there is a formal on-going system in place to combat it. Something is therefore needed for residential carers that would parallel the support given to foster carers.

This led us once more to reflect on the contrast we had experienced at the open forum between the confidence of the foster carers and the uncertainties of the residential carers. What emerged was a discrepancy between those who felt adequately trained, adequately supervised and adequately supported to undertake very difficult and demanding work, and those who did not. Status or qualification appeared less relevant than adequate consultation and space for reflection on work and feelings. If what we were seeing could be generalised to the service provision as a whole, the real demand from staff was for more help to do the work themselves, not a request to send children away to get specialist help. Without support, however, the task became so massive as to become unmanageable and, as a result, it evolved instead into a request for 'help specialists'.

It is therefore evident that there is a shared need for very similar support and training for existing workers, which might pre-empt some of the demand for specialist resources, while at the same time making it possible to identify more clearly the adolescents for whom a specialist resource of some kind might be desirable. This led us to consider the possibility of shared training for all carers, in a system and a structure of consultancy available to all workers with adolescents in care, wherever they were placed.

The Children Act

When the group embarked upon the research, the Children Act was on the distant horizon, and as we concluded the research implementation of the Act loomed closer. It has been a point of reference throughout, and our thoughts about the impact the Act will have on young people in care have changed as the detail of the legislation has emerged and as other related issues have advanced or receeded. There are uncertainties about the impact that the ethos of 'Care in the Community' will have on residential care for children; the only reliable guess one can make is that it will vary from one local authority to another. Of one aspect, however, we felt certain; which is that the emphasis in the legislation on taking the Act as a whole rather than in its separate parts, and the emphasis on partnership with parents, imply a major refocusing of the social work task and of social workers' attitudes. Partnership with parents implies wider partnerships; it implies partnership of parents with carers and it implies partnership between field social workers and carers. This will affect the status of both residential social workers and foster carers and could entail a wider sharing and a wider participation in decision-making. It raises questions about how and where decisions should be made about young people coming into care and about their placement. Who should be involved in these decisions? This will entail considerable changes in status and responsibility.

The Children Act promotes the idea of care as a resource for parents; we felt that care should also, and more importantly, be seen as a resource for children. To enable that to happen, the *carers* have to be valued, supported and given status. There needs to be recognition of the stress of being a carer to abused and desparate young people and recognition of what this implies — a need for support, for training and for space to reflect on what is happening and what it means to the worker and to the child.

Recommendations and conclusions
Some of our recommendations follow very directly from the research outlined above, some require more explanation and development.

1. Statistics
The main task of our research was to locate the population group we should be studying. The way information was held did not enable managers and workers to use it to understand the needs of the population they were dealing with. We felt that the reasons for which statistical information was held need to be reviewed in order for it to allow better analyses of the care population.

2. Accommodated children
At present the proportions of abused young people in voluntary and statutory care are about the same. If one of the aims of the Children Act is to avoid the unnecessary reception of children and young people into *statutory* care, then at least as many young people will be 'accommodated' by the local authority as are at present in voluntary care. There is no reason to suppose that there will be any change in the proportion of abused youngsters, so provision for 'accommodated' children and young people will equally need to have the capability to work effectively with the survivors of abuse.

3. Consultancy and resource information

We arrived at the recommendation that the department should set up a system of consultancy services for all workers in residential and day-care settings and for foster carers as well. In order to maintain itself as a strategic resource and avoid being eroded by other demands on the workers' time, it would have to be a section in its own right, separate from the main child care organisational structures.

This approach to supporting workers is not new and is the basis of many staff consultancy schemes; these are, however, frequently hard to sustain and liable to vanish if there are cuts, changes of personnel, or changes in management style or policy. It is for this reason that it should be 'institutionalised'. Suggesting that money be expended on such a resource in a period of severe financial restraint meant that we risked the reaction that we were living in 'cloud cuckoo land'. To suggest an initiative which would divert resources from front line child-protection work increased this risk. And yet report after report on child protection emphasises that effective work is only possible with effective supervision and support. While some of these reports may see supervision in largely managerial terms, others look on supervision as something concerned with extending the workers' ability to meet their client's needs while preventing them from becoming enmeshed in the client's problems. This is the nature of the work we would expect to be undertaken in consultancy. Such work suffers from the same problem as all preventative work, in that if it is effective, its impact is 'invisible'.

Not all children's needs can be met within the local authority child care system and there will always be some who need something different. There is a need to hold information about specialist resources (both residential and non-residential) for those children whose needs require them. The scarcity and expense of these resources needs to be recognised and their usefulness evaluated. We felt that this required a worker who was able to concentrate on this task without being deflected by short-term or crisis demands. As we discovered, this information is in a perpetual state of flux and very hard to evaluate. It requires a proactive seeking out of information, not only from the agencies concerned, but from the social workers who may most recently have had experience of them (and this in itself is difficult to discover). When the cost of some of these resources is considered, it seems reasonable to suggest that some money should be spent on ensuring that they are used properly. There would seem to be a value in linking this work with the work of a consultancy team, to ensure that there is a structured feedback between local and specialist resource systems.

Understanding the contradictions

Why did it feel like a revelation when our findings disclosed that a high proportion of adolescents in care had been abused? It seemed that everybody 'knew it', but that this knowledge went against the perceived idea that children in care are no different from children who are not in care — just more socially deprived. What we started to realise was that this put workers into a fundamental double bind; perhaps it even underlay the difficulty we had encountered in considering the provision of appropriate services for these adolescents.

Reflections on the research process

This chapter describes the research done by the project team and the issues and recommendations which evolved from the team's work. This final section, however, is a result of the two researchers from the West London Institute having had the task of putting pen to paper and, in the process, finding ourselves reflecting on the entire experience from a participant/observer stance. In some ways our position, as the 'researchers'; as distinct from practitioners, in the project team paralleled the role of the consultative team we eventually recommended. It is from our location both inside and outside the team and the child-care system that this section is written.

In retrospect, one of the most extraordinary aspects of our project group was how the process mirrored the content. By so doing it adds, in our view, both a further dimension of understanding to, and a confirmation of, the group's conclusions.

In the first instance, the task itself was plainly, like the social workers and researchers involved, over-ambitious and under-resourced. And like the task itself, the extent of the problem was unknown but was treated as if it were known.

At the initial stage, we felt separate from the group, and it was clear that the group was constituted of several sub-groups representing individuals with differing perspectives and interests. Within the group the competing demands on members' energy and attention mirrored the struggles within an SSD between the needs of different parts of the child care system.

Although our brief was to look at the care experience of adolescents who had been abused, and what could be done to improve the service, it took us many meetings before we could actually focus on the children in care! It seemed that first, the group had to work through an 'obsession' with the process of entry into the care system before any of us could begin to work on what happened to the children once in the system. For example, one aspect of our brief was to compare the careers of children in the system with those at risk at home. This led us down the path of concentrating on the distinction between staying out of and entering the care system. Thus we got sidetracked onto the process of entering the system rather than what was happening to the young people who had, for whatever reason, entered it. It was as if we all in turn struggled with an underlying ideology which was opposed to children coming into care and, as such, there was a preoccupation with the decision-making process by which children got there and were then placed in either residential or foster care. In spite of a brief which was very clearly to look at services for children who were in care, the focus returned repeatedly to how those children got into care. This remained a preoccupation which we never completely left behind, as can be seen from some of the information the group later collected, although the group (ourselves included) did not see that at the time. For example, half of the questions in our questionnaire (designed to elicit information about children already in care) were about what happened prior to their reception into care. In designing the questionnaire the group was unable to detach itself from this preoccupation.

Another example of this process was the early resignation from the group of the child protection specialist, whose main interest, inevitably, was gatekeeping entry to the care system. Although he was genuinely interested in what happened to the children in care, he was too pressured for time to attend this research project group concerning itself with service provision after the fact of entry.

There is a powerful body of social work opinion and research that aims to inhibit the entry of children into care, arising from the belief that many children are taken into care needlessly (DHSS 1986). While historically this may well be the case, what was significant about our findings was that they indicated that there was, prima facie, reason enough for young people in care to be there. 'Care', although inadequate, may be better than the situations from which they were removed. If we accept that the local authority is operating a 'good enough' system of gatekeeping entry into care, and not taking children into care whose only 'problem' is that their families are materially disadvantaged or culturally misunderstood, then the thrust of planning for these young people should not only be about preventing them coming into care but also about planning a *service* for them once there.

What the research group came to realise, when members discussed the findings, was that part of the reason we ourselves had become stuck on the issue of entry into care instead of thinking about the provision of care services was that we shared the general social work ambivalence about young people being 'in care'. Perhaps we could elucidate this with the following example.

In the 1960s, many children and young people entered residential care coming from families which were split up because of homelessness. Women were sent to one hostel, men to another, and the children were taken into care. The trauma for the child resulted from being separated from their families. The realisation that families, which could have been seen as 'good-enough' families, were being broken up by social circumstances drove social workers to strive harder to keep children out of care by supporting these families. 'Radical non-intervention', coupled with campaigns around family rights, emerged as a popular response. Eventually social policies and the law were changed in order to prevent young people entering care because of homelessness, in recognition that care as a response to homelessness was not only not good enough, it was bad for children.

In the 1990s fewer children and young people enter residential care, and if they do the reason is less likely to be so directly related to poverty. When the unemployed man was evicted 30 years ago his children went into care. Now the family will go into bed and breakfast. If, depressed and hopeless, he lashes out violently at his children, they too, like their counterparts 30 years ago are taken into care. But the trauma for the child is not only about being separated from the family, but also about having been the victim of family violence. The experience of that child, and the long-term effects of the abuse are different, even though the precipitating factor was a social problem. Thus we are faced with the phenomenon of 'victimising families' who are themselves victims of social problems.

Not able to prevent the moment when the victim becomes the victimiser, social workers get caught by their resistance to 'blaming' the victims; thus by their attempt to 'normalise' the experience of being in care, social workers must deny at some level that the reality for many young people in care is that their experiences are not 'normal'. Taught the implications of labelling, workers struggle to avoid labelling adolescents in care. Instead, this sometimes leads them to deny that there is a problem which needs resolution.

If this analysis corresponds with reality it is crucial to reiterate that with the implementation of the Children Act, there will be an implicit imperative for workers to treat accommodated children as qualitatively different from children in care; ie to see 'accommodated' children as being in care due to social circumstances, and children in statutory care as perhaps comprising the core of abused children. This denies the interrelatedness between the two and flies in the face of our findings which suggest that adolescents and children in *both* voluntary and statutory care are more likely than not to have been abused. Therefore, all care for young people, accommodated or statutory, must be 'good-enough' for abused children.

Again, in the open forum, process reflected content. Like children keeping the secret of abuse for fear that they would either not be believed, that the statement of fact would trigger disastrous consequences, or that everyone would be too overwhelmed by its impact to manage it helpfully, the workers perhaps have kept their suspicions secret. Having been given an opportunity in the open forum to express their belief that the majority of children in care had been abused, they were then freed to discuss what they did with that knowledge. A most fruitful dialogue arose between residential workers, foster carers and field workers during the ensuing exercise. Having aired this 'open secret', the two groups of carers (residential social workers and foster parents) were able to work together openly and constructively in discussing case examples, and looking at their commonalities.

The one residential social worker member of the research group dropped out as well. It seemed to us to reflect some of the difficulties in communication between the residential and fieldwork systems themselves. This left the project team in the strange situation of being a group discussing childen in care without any actual carers. The group recruited two foster carers who were of great importance to the group; but their position in the group, as members recruited after the start, could be seen to mirror the usual anomalous position of foster carers.

The senior social worker from the family therapy centre also had an interesting relationship to the project team. His professional interest in the group had been triggered by a commitment to a particular style of working with abused adolescents and he was in the early stages of setting up a pilot consultancy project with one of the children's homes. Although he dropped out of the ongoing work of the project team, he kept in close contact with us to share his consultancy experiences. The fact that as the 'specialist' in working with abused children he was part of, yet separate from, the project team mirrored in an interesting way the debate about the implications of the research findings.

If one considers this in relation to work with the young people themselves, then the changing population of the group could mirror the high turnover of staff. It is no wonder that plans for children and work with them gets disrupted. Part of the work of the recommended consultancy team would, of necessity, concern *holding* the knowledge about the child's behaviour throughout — despite changes in workers.

Finally, the fact that the researchers had to leave the system in order to reflect upon its functioning reinforces the argument for consultation. While we were actively in the group, we became as absorbed in the dynamics of the work as our project colleagues. This said, inasmuch as becoming immersed in the problems of practice temporarily impaired our capacity to analyse the situation, without such saturation and the opportunity to work alongside our colleagues in the field we would have learned little of value. As Parton (1989) observes:

> The best way of seeing research is as an aid to enlightenment and not as providing the answers. Practitioners and clients are the best experts on their problems so researchers need to make a greater effort to learn from and listen to, practice.

Once you start to consider research as something more than the collecting of facts, the potential complexities are manifest. We felt that in looking at the way in which the *content* of the research material was mirrored in the research *process*, we were beginning to explore one of these complexities. The experimental nature of the research method seems to us to have opened up new aspects of the research process. Our observations on the process were both unexpected and exciting and lead us to hope that we can explore this aspect of research methodology further.

References

DHSS 1986 *Decision Making in Child Care*. HMSO

Docker-Drysdale B 1968 *Therapy in Child Care*. Longmans

Durrant M 1987 Therapy with young people who have been the victims of sexual assault. In *Family Therapy Care Studies* 2 (1). Eastwood Centre

George E, Iveson C, Ratner H 1990 *Problems to Solution: Brief Therapy with Individuals and Families*. BT Press

Menzies I 1970 *The Functioning of Social Systems as a Defence Against Anxiety*. Tavistock Institute. Recently republished in *Containing Anxiety in Institutions* (1988). Free Associations Press

Parton N 1989 Child abuse. In Kahan B *Child Care Research, Policy and Practice*. Hodder & Stoughton

Pettican K, Turner P 1984 Fostering abused children. *Foster Care* 37 March

Roberts J 1986 Fostering the sexually abused child. *Adoption and Fostering* **10** (1)

4 Preparation for poverty: rethinking residential care

Mike Allin, David Barrett, Hamish Canham, Gill Harris, Nick Moore, John Pitts, Steve Tall, Rinske Taekema and Clare Walker

> This chapter considers the current state of residential care for young people and the ways in which the decline of the 'residential solution' and the rise of 'community care' have worsened the predicament of the young people who remain in local authority residential establishments. It examines aspects of the residential services for young people in one local authority and ends with a discussion of the ways in which residential care for young people might be transformed into a positive choice.

In the autumn of 1990 young people in care hit the headlines once again. This time, in the wake of the *Sunday Correspondent* exposé of a South London children's home, questions were asked in parliament and the Minister of State, Virginia Bottomley, instituted an enquiry, undertaken by the Social Services Inspectorate, into residential provision for adolescents in London.

In fact, the tales of drug-taking, crime and prostitution recounted by the *Correspondent*, alarming though they were, are relatively innocuous when set against the many other scandals, Kincora being the most notorious, which have rocked residential work in the past decade [*Sunday Correspondent* 1990].

These incidents raise many questions about the management of residential establishments and the recruitment, selection, training and support of staff. They also reveal a widespread confusion about the purpose of residential care and the rights and obligations of staff, residents and local authorities.

Sadly, these questions tend to be addressed only when things go wrong. Indeed, for the past decade the debate about residential work with adolescents seems to have been couched almost entirely in negative terms. It is our belief, however, that if we can find an answer to the question 'what would residential work with adolescents look like if it was going right?', things would go wrong far less often.

In our view, such positive practice must be rooted in a clarity on the part of the local authority about what it means to assume responsibility for parenting deprived and neglected young people.

What is a 'good enough' local authority?

The 1989 Children Act enjoins local authority social workers to place children and young people in care only if such a placement will cause less harm than would be caused by leaving them in their own homes. This enshrines in law what usually happens in practice and defines a negative minimum standard.

However, a responsible local authority will strive to provide more than a situation in which neglect or abuse are simply absent. The local government Ombudsman's report on abuses at a Greenwich children's home [1990, p60] expresses the view that:

> Children in care have often come from insecure and unstable backgrounds. They have the right to expect that council homes will provide a caring and stable environment.

Chapter 3 of this book reveals that the majority of young people entering the care system in the authority where this study was conducted had been abused and Chapter 6 indicates that they were also economically and socially deprived and subject to racial discrimination. As such, they were a group of people demonstrably in need of such a caring and stable environment.

The provision of caring and stability is however a formidable task. It involves addressing neglect or abuse with a young person and attempting to repair the damage it has wrought in their lives. It involves offering them 'treatment' if this is appropriate and providing the positive, 'compensatory' experiences and relationships which constitute such care and stability. The 'good enough' local authority must therefore strive to do this if it is to provide a 'good enough' environment for neglected or abused children and young people.

While it would be a mistake to suggest that there was ever a 'golden age' of residential work in which all of these objectives were fulfilled, it is nonetheless clear that political and economic changes in the past decade or so have eroded the ability of local authorities to fulfil their obligations to young people in residential care.

Ironically, their predicament has sometimes been worsened by the development of community-based alternatives to residential care.

The advent of community care

Until the early 1980s, government polices for residential child care were formulated in isolation from, or as a minor appendage of, mainstream health and welfare policies. The world was effectively divided into two. There were residential institutions and beyond them an amorphous terrain called 'the community' whose defining characteristic was that it was not a residential institution. The notion that the residential institution might be part of, draw upon or contribute to, 'the community' is a comparatively recent one (Wagner 1988, Griffith 1988).

Such separate treatment of residential institutions and their residents can be traced back variously to the Elizabethan poor law and to what Foucault (1977) describes as the 'great confinement', that period at the end of the 18th and the beginning of the 19th century in North Western Europe which witnessed the widescale expulsion of the mad, the delinquent, paupers and orphans to large institutions beyond the city limits. The social marginality of these people was compounded by the stigma associated with the institutions in which they were held.

150 years later the pendulum was swinging away from institutional solutions. This reversal was a product of the mounting professional and academic critique of residential care, growing pressure across a broad political spectrum for the recognition of children's rights, political hostility to state intervention and, perhaps most importantly, a fiscal crisis in central and local government which was pricing the residential solution out of the market (Bowlby 1971, Cornish and Clarke 1975, Millham et al. 1978, Scull 1977).

This crisis meant that many local authorities closed their children's homes, developed adolescent fostering services, supported voluntary organisations which were providing community alternatives to residential care and custody for young offenders and, where possible, sub-contracted residential child-care to private and voluntary organisations (Holroyd 1983, Bernstein 1984, Nellis 1989). In this way, local authorities attempted to discharge their responsibility to offer neglected or abused children and young people care and stability. There is evidence to suggest that in many cases, adolescent fostering being a case in point, this responsibility was discharged satisfactorily. In some other cases however, it was not.

A placement for the hard to place

As a result of these developments the number of young people in local authority residential care has been significantly reduced. Those who can be placed elsewhere have been. Those young

Preparation for poverty 59

people who remain in local authority residential provision tend, therefore, either to be there as a result of short-term 'emergency admissions' or they are part of the 'hard-to-place' residue whose placements 'break down' or who persistently abscond from other placements.

The problems of working with these young people are exacerbated by the, usually unacknowledged, political and professional values which inform both attitudes and resource allocation in local authorities.

These values can be expressed as a series of propositions:

1. The best possible place for a child or young person to live is with their own family.
2. The second best place for a child or young person to live is with a foster family.
3. The worst place for a child or young person to live is in a residential institution.

A few moments thought reveal some serious problems with this ostensibly straightforward account of what constitutes a child or young person's best interest. Many responsible parents struggle long and hard, sometimes taking on additional jobs, to pay for their child to be placed in a residential institution. For them, sending their child away to public school is a positive choice. Many relatively privileged young people are eager to get to College or University, not simply to be exposed to new ideas but because they want freedom from their families; freedom to live in a residential institution, called a hall of residence, with other young people. It is at least unlikely that many of them would want to trade life in the institution for a substitute family which would offer them a quasi-parental relationship. For them, the residential institution is a positive choice. The obvious difference between these residential institutions and most local authority provision for adolescents is that they have high status and residence in them is part of a process in which people's life-chances are substantially enhanced.

As Chapter 3 reveals, the majority of young people entering care have been abused. In some cases the brutality or sexual exploitation took place in their family and was inflicted upon them by parents or step-parents. As David Crimmens notes in Chapter 7, far from wanting or needing a substitute family, some of these young people want some respite from the anxiety they feel about the destructive intimacy of family relationships. For them as well, residential care is a positive choice.

But they are inserted into a system in which the residential institution is regarded as the least desirable option, in which entry to that institution signals either a failure on the part of the young person to 'make it' at home or in a 'better' placement, or a failure on the part of their field social worker who should have been able to keep them there.

The low-status of the provision is reflected in the poor state of repair of many residential institutions, the low status of staff vis-à-vis their community-based counterparts, their low level of training and support and their low pay. The consequent high staff turnover leads to frequent vacancies and this shortfall is made up by agency staff who work on a sessional basis, thus contributing further to the instability of these institutions. How, we might ask, can we develop a caring response to neglected young people if the places in which this caring is to be done and the people who are to do it are themselves uncared for and neglected.

The Wagner Report

It was to some of these problems that the Wagner Report *A Positive Choice* (1988) was a response. Wagner emphasised the need to transform residential care into something which would be regarded by those who provided it, and the deprived and damaged young people who entered it, as something more than preparation for the dole queue. This could be achieved, Wagner argued, through establishing a clear charter of residents' rights and care providers' responsibilities.

To an extent Wagner represented a rearguard defence of professional social work values against the onslaught of economic pragmatism in the guise of community care. The report acknowledged what it describes as the 'new economics' but stopped well short of a Griffith-style wholehearted embrace:

> ... efficiency, effectiveness and economy. These are no Thatcherite ephemera or ceremonial paraphernalia. They are already, and will surely remain, fundamental institutional reminders of the 'new economics of social care'.

Wagner echoes a key theme in the 1989 Children Act in its transformation of the *client* into a *resident* and its emphasis on the *partnership* which should exist between care providers and a young person in residential care. Such partnership offers a basis upon which the gradual transfer of power and autonomy from the one to the other implied in the Gillick judgement might be achieved (*Regina* v *Gillick* 1988).

The barriers to a positive choice

It is evident that if residential care is to be a positive choice for young people it must first become a positive choice for local authority councillors, managers and practitioners. In the present study, aspects of which are reported here, we attempted to identify variations in standards of provision for adolescents in care in one local authority. This constitutes the first step towards the broader task of specifying what would constitute a minimum standard which a local authority in its role as 'good enough parent' should be aiming to achieve. It is noteworthy that before undertaking the study a number of other local authorities were approached for advice. None of them had conducted such a review themselves nor were they aware of any other authority which had.

In the 1980s the social services department in which the study was undertaken began to consider the principles and values which should underpin good childcare practice in general and work with adolescents in particular. These deliberations were eventually published in its Children and Families Policy.

The central tenets of this policy are that a young person should, wherever practicable, be diverted from reception into care. If, however, they are at risk of serious emotional, sexual or physical harm they should be taken into care and the care experience should constitute a positive benefit to them. Such positive benefit is to be achieved by, wherever possible, placing a young person in an adolescent fostering placement, enabling them to maintain links with their family of origin, keeping sibling groups together and working towards rehabilitation with their family of origin. If this is not possible then substitute family care is to be sought. Taken together, these principles are seen to constitute the 'best interests of the child'.

In practice, however, there are substantial barriers to the pursuit of such 'best interest'. These barriers are most evident in the areas of occupancy, staffing, money and building maintenance.

Occupancy

1. Keeping families together

Sometimes, a large family with children whose ages range from 9 or 10 to 15 or 16 is received into care. Large families are hard to foster in a single placement and so, if the sibling group is to be kept together, the obvious solution would be a placement in a residential establishment.

The closure of some children's homes in the borough in recent years means that the remaining provision usually has a relatively high occupancy level. Establishments are designated for children under 11 or for young people over 11 and staff are recruited to work with one group or the other. The equipment in these establishments, beds, cupboards, toys and books are similarly age-specific.

Good practice and departmental policy dictate that siblings should be placed together but limited capacity and high occupancy mean that this is not possible. These problems are compounded by the ways in which the quality of the service is evaluated. The performance indicators currently in use are based solely on occupancy. High occupancy equals good practice, low occupancy equals bad practice. This emphasis on filling beds means that the professional, and indeed policy, considerations are subordinated to financial ones. It is clear therefore that a prerequisite of good practice as defined in the *Children and Families Policy* is that there should be more slack in the system.

2. Maintaining family links

Policy notwithstanding, there are no community or assessment foster placements within the borough and only one long-term residential establishment. Short-term provision is available within the borough but high occupancy levels often mean that young people in crisis will be placed in private and voluntary provision outside the borough or in bed and breakfast accommodation. While this is not a pressing problem for all local authorities it is one which confronts many London boroughs.

In short, the chances of a young person in the care of the authority remaining in the borough are slim. Only if they are fortunate enough to be placed in the one long-term unit in the borough, if they are placed in a short-term unit and return home, if they are placed in bed and breakfast or if they abscond from an out-of-borough placement can they remain in the borough.

This is clearly very disruptive. Many children and young people in care are poor school attenders and a transfer to a new area is often sufficient to transform a poor attender into a non-attender. More importantly, the ties with their family, often weak at the best of times, are stretched even further by a move outside the borough. The policy document recognises the high priority which should be given to the maintenance of such family ties. Pitts (1990, p124) writes:

> Though less obviously dependent on their families than younger children, and even though they might be in conflict with their parents, they badly need a family to re-enter. Our job in this situation is to so organise things between the child or young person, the parents and brothers and sisters and the residential, home or foster-parents that families which have difficulty with the mechanics of caring, or don't actually care very much, are enabled to express that care to the child or young person as regularly and as often as possible. Sometimes the maintenance of affectional bonds presents itself to us as an organisational problem.

This organisational problem is made doubly difficult by the placement of most of the adolescent in-care population outside the borough. Parents whose children are in care often feel a sense of guilt, failure and inadequacy and these feelings create additional barriers to contact. Whereas more contact might help to lessen these feelings, the monthly travel warrant to visit a child seems, if anything, to deepen them.

3. Dealing in diversity

The progressive intentions of the Children and Families Policy notwithstanding, there is no mechanism for matching residential provision with the needs and practices of the racial, religious and cultural groups who make up the population of the area served. As Chapter 6 indicates, Morrocan and Afro-Carribean/Black British youngsters are heavily over-represented in the local care and juvenile justice systems. The maintenance of links with the local community are of considerable importance to Afro-Carribean young people and of particular importance to Morrocan youngsters since, although the Morrocan community in the borough is small, in the rest of the city it is effectively non-existent. A long-term strategy to institutionalise an ethnically-sensitive practice and managerial strategy in residential work with children and young people is therefore required. Cheetham (Ahmet et al. 1986, p119) observes that:

> ... establishing ethnic issues as part of normal review procedures and taking account of their importance in planning for black children in care cannot be done through an isolated exercise.

Staffing

One of the consequences of the development of community fostering and intensive IT in recent years has been that although a smaller number of young people are entering residential care, their problems are more serious. The unmanageable South London children's home featured in the *Correspondent* article, cited above, was not untypical in terms of the type of problems confronting residential workers. Placing a number of damaged and vulnerable young people together can also mean that, without careful handling, a volatile group can become an unmanageable one.

Though smaller in number, the nature of the problems presented by young people in residential care suggest that a more generous staff ratio is required if their needs are to be met. But staff establishment is determined on the basis of the capacity of residential units rather than the complexity of the tasks to be undertaken in them. Beyond this, as large establishments have been shut and smaller ones retained, the per capita cost of a residential placement has rocketed. This has caused cost-conscious councillors to view arguments about improved staff ratios with scepticism and, thus far, professionals and managers have failed to win this argument with their political masters.

With the closure of establishments and the reduction in the size of those which remain, the size of staff groups has been reduced. As a result of this, and changed shift patterns, it is common practice for two staff to be on duty over a 24-hour period. These staff are supplemented by agency workers if the unit has particular needs or faces particular difficulties.

Permanent staffing levels are determined on the basis of the minimum number of people needed to cover the hours in the week but no allowance is made in this calculation for sickness, training, holidays and vacancies. These 'gaps' are covered by agency staff but it requires only one or two vacancies and a few members of staff to be on holiday or off sick for most of the borough's homes to be staffed by temporary agency workers. This is not unusual, many local authorities staff their residential services in this way.

As a result, rather than contributing to the caring and stable environment commended by the Ombudsman, this staffing strategy contributes to instability and discontinuity of care. To this extent agency staff, irrespective of their skills and abilities, but because of the ways in which they are used, are sometimes part of the problem rather than part of the solution.

As Chapter 6 notes, sometimes the most effective work with young people will be done on an outreach basis by a worker with whom they have developed a close relationship. Indeed, effective outreach can sustain young people in the community who would otherwise have to be taken back into residential care. In terms of the best interest of a child or young person and as a cost-effective response, this is clearly a desirable practice. Yet, not only does a minimum-cover staffing strategy work against both the possibility of developing such a close relationship and finding time to engage in outreach work, but performance indicators, by rewarding high occupancy levels, fail to support such initiatives.

Relatively low salaries and unsocial hours lead to difficulties in recruiting permanent staff. This is compounded by the peculiar difficulties of attracting social work staff to London. Although training budgets have grown in recent years, secondment to professional training courses has ceased and so a traditional source of permanent staff, people gaining experience in residential work while waiting for the local authority to second them to a professional training course, has dried up. Residential work retains a low status within social work and despite the interpersonal skills

Money

Any attempt to address the quality of life of young people in residential care must consider the money given to or spent on them. There is a substantial difference in the personal allowances given to young people in different types of placement. The starkest contrast is between young people in adolescent fostering placements and those in residential care.

Table 4.1 illustrates clearly the differential payments made to young people in different types of placement. Historically allowances for young people in residential care have been uprated annually in line with inflation. There has been no review of what it actually costs to care for a young person or of the ways in which changes in fashion and improvements in standards of dress, holidays and recreational activities in the world beyond and children's home might affect these costs.

Table 4.1: Differential payments made to young people

	Community fostering (£)	Residential (£)
15 year old		
Pocket money	9.73	3.92
Clothing	14.70	7.95
Birthday	73.08	12.97
Christmas	73.08	12.97
Holiday	146.16	256.27
11 year old		
Pocket money	5.46	1.99
Clothing	13.51	4.71
Birthday	60.55	10.83
Christmas	60.55	10.83
Holiday	121.10	256.27
7 year old		
Pocket money	2.73	1.36
Clothing	10.29	4.71
Birthday	48.72	8.00
Christmas	48.72	8.00
Holiday	87.44	256.27

When compared with the more recently established adolescent fostering scheme in which the rates were calculated on the basis of a young person's needs in the late 1980s, residential care emerges as a very poor relation. This echoes the low value placed on residential care discussed above.

Whereas foster carers and social workers regard their allowances as adequate, neither group consider children's homes allowances to be so. Residential social workers admit that they have sometimes resorted to creative accounting in order to introduce some equity into the system. In one case in which a family was divided between a children's home and a community fostering placement workers and carers enabled the children in the foster placement to provide Christmas presents for their brothers and sisters out of the fostering allowance.

Residential establishments are required by the ordering systems of the local authority to buy many household items in bulk. This may be efficient and economical but it makes it difficult for young people to become involved in, and learn the skills of, housekeeping which they will eventually need far more than young people who are brought up in their own families.

Centralised administrative systems control the flow of money to residential establishments. Clothing grants must therefore be requested well in advance and spontaneous purchases, which are very important to young people, are hard to accommodate within the confines of petty cash. These bureaucratic restrictions mean that workers have burdensome procedures to go through to purchase even the smallest item for a young person. This is not the case for youngsters in foster placements. These bureaucratic systems were designed in an era when there was little recognition of the stigma of living in care or the need to prepare young people for independence. They reflect a widespread ambivalence and uncertainty about what residential care is supposed to be preparing young people for. Indeed it is sometimes argued that the quality of care should not accustom young people to a lifestyle they will be unable to sustain when they leave care or return to their family. If, however, we were to suggest that middle class parents should limit the amount they spend on their children's food, clothes and holidays in order to accustom them to the lifestyle of a hard-up student, this suggestion would, we imagine, be greeted with some scepticism.

There is evidence that some previously law-abiding young people in residential establishments have turned to petty theft in order to buy the extra clothes and pay for the outings which their school friends who live at home can afford as a matter of course. There must be something wrong with a child-care system which drives its subjects to crimes of poverty.

The differential treatment of young people in foster homes and residential placements continues throughout the system and beyond it. When a young person leaves care they are nominated for housing by the local authority. Young people in residential care are more likely to be nominated for a 'bedsit' than a flat. There is some evidence of discrimination in favour of fostered young people, who tend to be regarded by some housing officers as less potentially troublesome.

Building maintenance

The quality of their physical environment is important to most young people. Not only should they have a say in the ways in which their rooms are decorated and adorned, but the fabric of the building in which they live is also important. The quality of that fabric is dependent upon a sensitive bureaucratic response to the particular demands placed upon residential establishments. This requires an understanding of the social work task and what can happen to a building with 8 to 10 teenagers in it. A brief temper tantrum by a disturbed 16 year old can cause a great deal of very expensive damage yet it is in the nature of the work that incidents of this type will occur regularly.

Systems currently operating within the local authority take little or no account of the purpose for which buildings are used when apportioning money for repairs and redecoration. Each year a repairs budget is drawn up based on an average of the previous year's costs for a range of establishments plus an allowance for inflation. As a result the maintenance bills for units which house adolescents stand out as exceptional. There is often a feeling within the organisation that if only the workers had been more responsible or had exerted more control, such excesses need not have occurred. There is sometimes a feeling of exasperation and even outrage at such behaviour and a consequent reluctance to make good the damage it has wrought. It is difficult for key decision-makers both as politicians and managers and as human beings who may be parents or grandparents to accept the reality of seriously disturbed behaviour. Yet this is the reality of much contemporary residential work with young people and this failure to make an adequate response has meant that buildings are in a very poor state of repair. Such obvious neglect signals to the young people who live in them that the authority does not care about them and does not expect them to care about the buildings. It should come as no surprise therefore when they don't.

Building the foundations for a positive choice

Our study revealed gaps, sometimes large ones, between policy intentions and day-to-day practice and this suggests that policy does not, of itself, bring about change. To be effective policy must be supported by a strategy for change which identifies practical ways in which the gaps can be narrowed.

As has been argued above, any such strategy must proceed on the assumption that the young people entering residential care will have been abused and that because of this the local authority has a special responsibility to provide those resources and services which contribute to the development of a caring and stable environment. Such a strategy would involve gaining information about the needs of the people in the localities served by the authority. This would include information about the particular needs of the racial, religious and cultural groups in those localities. At present information on race and religion are not kept and this colour-blind approach means that it is impossible to monitor whether or not racism is institutionalised within the system.

While a useful complaints procedure exists there is, as yet, no charter of rights for young people in local authority residential care and such a charter, with a built-in monitoring system, would offer a helpful basis for the closer definition of minimum standards.

Our study focused particularly on four areas: occupancy, staffing, money and buildings. What then should the strategy for change in these areas be?

Occupancy

The question of occupancy offers a good example of a situation in which the right hand of the local authority is unaware of what the left hand is doing. The performance indicators for residential staff were formulated with an eye to the local authority's responsibility as judicious custodian of the public purse. The Children and Families Policy was formulated with an eye to the local authority's responsibility as responsible provider of a caring and secure environment for abused and neglected children and young people. However, in this case, the cheapest solution is obviously not the best one and this suggests that performance indicators should be developed which take cognisance of the imperatives of good child-care practice as well.

The rigid policy of dividing young people and institutions into age bands must be revised if the Children and Families Policy is to be adhered to. That policy would seem to indicate a more flexible use of existing provision which allows it to be adapted to the needs of sibling groups with a wide age range, even at the expense of high occupancy rates.

If the partnership between parents, children and the local authority envisaged in the 1989 Children Act, and the 'positive choice' espoused by Wagner (1988) are to become a reality the present system will not be adequate. If the local authority is to fulfil its duties to 'accommodated' children and young people and if they and their parents are to participate in decisions about allocation, more flexible use of existing provision and an extension of the range of provision will be necessary.

At present estimates for expenditure or residential care tend to be arrived at by reference to expenditure in neighbouring or comparable authorities. Only when the reference point shifts from a minimum standard established by custom and practice in local authorities to a specification of what constitutes the 'secure and caring' environment which it is incumbent on the local authority, as a 'good enough' parent, to provide, will progress be possible.

Staffing

Any charter of rights for young people in residential care must address the quality of the service they receive from staff. For abused and neglected young people, continuity of contact is of the utmost importance if they are to rebuild a capacity to trust. Clearly then, the local authority in its role as 'good enough' parent should underwrite such continuity. This would suggest a staffing policy based upon the need to undertake agreed tasks rather than the need to simply provide 'minimum cover'. Continuity might also be enhanced by the creation of a peripatetic team to cover vacancies and absences rather than the present, relatively expensive, practice of employing agency staff.

Money

The present discrepancies in allowances to young people in residential care and community fostering would make nonsense of any charter of rights. Allowances should simply be standardised and a coherent budgeting system, responsive to changing needs and changing standards, should be established.

The leaving-care allowance should be standardised to correspond with the present upper level and grants to enable young people to establish themselves in independent living should be determined on the basis that part of the authority's responsibility to them will be to help them find flats rather than 'bedsits'.

As Chapter 2 indicates, young people who have been through the care system are often seriously disadvantaged in their attempts to make an independent life for themselves. The National Children's Bureau briefing paper *Leaving Residential Care* (Robinson 1983) suggests that older children leaving care require:

1. preparation for independence while still in a residential home;
2. intermediate supported accommodation, and
3. help to establish themselves in good permanent accommodation;

this is however rarely achieved. It would not be the mark of a responsible parent that they ceased to be interested in, or offer support to, their child simply because their legal responsibility had ceased. Similarly, a responsible local authority would not abandon neglected or abused young people simply because they were no longer in care. It would therefore seem appropriate that local authorities should acknowledge a degree of financial responsibility for young people who have spent significant periods in their care. These older teenagers are still 'children in trust'.

Building maintenance

Devolved resource management (DRM) could provide an answer to the particular problems of maintaining the physical fabric of residential establishments at an acceptable level. DRM, like the local management of schools, involves the distribution to local level of all maintenance, building and supply functions. It would allow managers of residential establishments more control over these aspects of their work and so enable them to develop a more responsive and sensitive service for young people. If necessary, extra training and consultancy could be provided in areas like building maintenance where they may presently lack expertise.

For DRM to work, however, there needs to be an acknowledgement by councillors and senior managers of the peculiar, and often very expensive, demands which are placed upon residential establishments for young people.

Conclusion

Between the beginning of the 19th century and the early 1970s the residential child care system in Britain developed by a process of accretion, layer upon layer. New annexes were added to old buildings. Psychology and treatment were superimposed upon morality and discipline. Changing ideologies, policies and administrative systems were piled one on top of another.

From the early 1970s, a process of erosion was set in train in which residential nurseries, many community homes and most community homes with education, were closed down. Like an ancient cliff battered by the sea, the remnants of the system which nobody planned, nobody intended and nobody owns, stands with its layers exposed. As we discovered, when one tries to impose a progressive policy upon this system, based as it is on deeply buried values and the remnants of regressive bureaucratic practices, the rationale for which is lost in the mists of time, it will not work.

No wonder then that the local authority in its role as parent is confused. For almost two decades it has presided enthusiastically over the demolition of residential child care services and the development of 'community care'. As Kate Priestly (1990) of Newcastle SSD has observed,

> the only way we've been able to promote community care is at the expense of residential care.

This has meant that little if any choice is available to youngsters entering residential care. In Warwickshire, the wholesale closure of children's homes in 1986 has left the authority with no residential services of its own. David Cliffe (1990), who undertook a study in the wake of these developments notes that:

> most children were offered only one choice of foster placement and, obviously, no residential placement — in other words, no choice at all. Secondly, although Warwickshire has shown that more difficult children can be fostered than was previously thought, there is still a small group — mostly adolescent boys — who need residential placements.

In another authority in the South East of England, which had abandoned virtually all of its residential provision, some young people who persistently 'broke down' in adolescent fostering placements were referred to the county adolescent psychiatric unit because it was the only residential facility in the area.

Now the 1989 Children Act, with its emphasis upon residential care as a positive choice made on the basis of a partnership between the local authority and a young person, asks the local authority to specify a minimum level of provision and a minimum standard of practice.

Peter Elfer (1990) observes that as a result:

> senior managers and elected members have to recognise the duty of the LA under the Act to ensure minimum standards and give greater priority to the necessary management processes to support this.

Yet nobody needs reminding that high inflation and poll tax cutting or capping will mean that many SSDs face the prospect of losing several million pounds from their budgets.

What is needed now is not further administrative restructuring, the usual knee-jerk response to dwindling resources, but a change in local authority culture and values. Good quality residential care of the type that should be provided by a 'good enough' local authority requires financial and moral support from councillors, managers and professionals. If the recent British Social Attitudes survey (Jowell, Witherspoon and Brook 1990) is to be believed it already has this support from the public. Meanwhile local authorities are locked into the new economics where it remains to be seen if the political rhetoric which characterises the 1990s as the caring decade will be translated into action. The ruthless pursuit of economic rationality in health, education and welfare services may have run its course and while the recent resignation of Margaret Thatcher does not necessarily signal the end of the economic rationalism characteristic of Thatcherism, it may presage an era in which concerns about the quality of the lives of our most vulnerable citizens is put back on the political agenda.

As we have tried to suggest, 'quality of life' is more than a vague assertion about the importance of individual well-being. It manifests itself in concrete terms, in occupancy levels, staffing, pocket money and the presence of absence of minimum standards. As such it can be monitored and such monitoring by producing measurable outcomes can lay the basis for an accountable service (Baldwin, Godfrey and Propper 1990). Virginia Bottomley, on behalf of the government, is resisting pressure to establish national minimum standards for the residential care of young people. If, therefore, minimum standards are to be established, it will be done through collaboration between practitioners, managers and the local politicians who will, or will not, choose to be 'good enough' parents.

References

Ahmet S, Cheetham J, Small J (eds) 1986 *Social Work with Black Children and their Families*. Batsford
Baldwin S, Godfrey C, Propper C, 1990 *Quality of Life*. Routledge
Bernstein M 1984 Something will turn up. *Community Care* 6 September
Bowlby J 1971 *Attachment*. Pelican
Cliffe D 1990 Warwickshire's minefield *Community Care* 25 October
Commission for Local Administration in England 1990 *Report of the Local Ombudsman on an Investigation into Complaints against the London Borough of Greenwich*
Cornish D, Clarke R 1975 *Residential Treatment and its Effects on Delinquency*. Home Office
Elfer P 1990 Their need — our future *Community Care* 20 October
Foucault M 1977 *Discipline and Punishment*. Allen Lane, Penguin Books
Griffith R 1988 *Community Care: An Agenda for Action*. HMSO
Holroyd D 1983 Service purchase — what it can do for a department. *Municipal Journal* 2 December
Jowell, Witherspoon, Brook 1990 *7th British Social Attitudes Survey*. Gower
Millham S, Bullock R, Hosie K 1978 *Locking Up Children*. Saxon House
Nellis M 1989 Juvenile justice and the voluntary sector. In Matthews R (ed) *Privatising Criminal Justice*. Sage
Pitts J 1990 *Working with Young Offenders*. BASW/Macmillan

Priestley K 1990 Feeling the strain. *Community Care* 20 October
Robinson J 1983 *Leaving Residential Care*. National Children's Bureau
Scull A 1977 *Decarseration: Community Treatment and the Deviant*. Prentice Hall
Sunday Correspondent 1990 The lost children of Grove Park. 30 September
Wagner G 1988 *A Positive Choice*. National Institute of Social Work

5 The mother of invention — negative reform and secure accommodation

John Dennington

> This chapter suggests that while the introduction of court proceedings to determine access to secure accommodation has formally provided a more rigorous 'gate', this has not prevented security being used inappropriately. It considers whether recent calls by government, that local authorities should themselves impose better controls on admissions, will stop this continuing misuse. It goes on to compare the activities of three social services departments in relation to the use of secure accommodation.

Every year across this country nearly two thousand young people are locked up in secure accommodation. Some are there for very short periods while others are detained longer. However, all have their liberty withdrawn and all are exposed to the criminalising effects of institutional life under lock and key. About a quarter are held on remand awaiting trial for serious crimes, although a sizeable number are subsequently found not guilty, but others may have committed no crime at all and are held because they are absconders thought to be at risk of 'significant harm' or because it is believed they are likely to injure themselves or others. Apart from the three per cent who are detained under Section 53 for having committed grave offences, secure accommodation is reserved for children in care. Troubled and difficult youngsters who stay out of the care system are not eligible for secure provision. Set against this is the powerful irony that those children who may perhaps have come into 'voluntary' care as a result of family problems can end up locked up in a secure unit. The inequity behind the fact that it is only those vulnerable young people in care, who can be treated in this way is self-evident and raises the important civil liberties question of why this group, alone of all young people, should be selected to have their freedom threatened by special laws applied just to them.

The development of the secure option

Encouraged by government grants, secure accommodation expanded dramatically in the 1970s. Over fifteen million pounds was granted to local authorities from 1976 to encourage them to develop more of this provision, inspiring a rise in secure places to a peak of 430 in 1981.

A rapid expansion took place against an ideological backdrop which asserted that young people in the care system were becoming *more* difficult, and that therefore more specialised provision was needed to contain, and work with, the youngsters with whom the mainstream care system could not. Millham (1978), a major contributor to the debate about security in the 1970s, astutely observed though that:

> ... these units are largely employed in meeting the problem behaviour that threatens the well-being of *other* residential institutions.

The research which monitored and reviewed the usage to which the new service was put reached some disquieting conclusions. Despite the fact that the creation of secure provision had been justified on the basis of the argued need for containment of those youngers in care with the most acute presenting problems, the research revealed a tendency of closed units to reject the most difficult youngsters and instead draw in less problematic children with 'milder' problems. Paradoxically, many of the older youngsters in the care system eventually found themselves in the borstals and, with this group hived off into the penal system, secure units tended to take younger, 'disturbed' children with histories of absconding. An 'experiment that cannot fail' was therefore set up. Once the assertion that there was a core of problem children in care had been accepted, the units were built. Once there, they were of course available to be used. Youngsters were subsequently referred to the units, in many cases inappropriately, but the fact that these units were being utilised meant that to many in the social work field their existence was justified. This led Cawson and Martell (1979) to note:

> ... closed provision was justified in terms of its *use*: the fact that children were being referred and admitted showed that there was a continuing need for children to be placed in closed conditions. The dangers of this process are evident. It provides a formula for the justification of a service regardless of any necessity to demonstrate its value or effectiveness.

However, despite the tendency to attract less problematic, inappropriate admissions the glut of new units nevertheless found themselves 'struggling' (sic) with some of the more difficult residents and, true to the tradition of British institutional containment, there developed an increasing pressure for closed units that were even more intensive. The Youth Treatment Centre was born. As Millham (1978) says:

> Yet another institutional answer was offered to an institutional problem. ... The strength of the institutional tradition meant that answers to difficulties were always sought in institutional contexts.

Commentators, observing that many of the young people so placed did not truly warrant secure containment, suggest that secure accommodation serves as a kind of 'expansion tank' for the care system. It acts to catch on 'overflow' of problematic youngsters who do not fit in to the limited range of mainstream care facilities on offer. In this way, the use of secure accommodation by a local authority can perhaps be seen as an indicator that may say more about the resilience of that authority's care services at any one time than about the pathology of those individual clients locked up by it. As one recent article put it (Allen and Hill 1990):

> The use of secure care is really dependent on what is beside it; what kind of residential care, what kind of preventive services, what sort of policies and practices with children and young people in care and with juvenile offenders.

The courts get involved — impartial arbiter or rubber stamp?

As a result of pressure from social work academics and practitioners, concern over the immoderate use of security eventually resulted in the implementation, in May 1983, of Section 21A of the Child Care Act 1980 and the associated Secure Accommodation Regulations 1983. Henceforth it would only be possible to place a child in security with the agreement of a court. Nevertheless, while these limitations introduced for the first time some criteria against which to judge if a youngster should be admitted, the introduction of a more formal process overseeing entry into security has not had the expected impact anticipated. The magistracy, which was inserted into the process to 'gatekeep' access to secure accommodation, has emerged for the main part as a device for confirming local authority recommendations. This tendency has led one researcher, when reviewing the impact of the magistrates' new powers and responsibilities, to observe (Holden 1985):

> A reasonably conscientious care authority has little to fear from these procedures. The number of applications which have been refused have been very small. There may have been some reluctance to consider secure accommodation in some cases where it would otherwise have been used, because of the necessity of taking the

case before the court, and to that extent the procedures will have been effective.

So, while the new legal mechanisms have surely required local authorities to consider applications for security with more care and to carefully collate their arguments for presentation to a court, the real power determining who goes into secure accommodation remains relatively unchanged, such that (DoH 1990):

> Once the departmental decision has been made to 'go for secure' there is a very good chance that an authorisation will be granted.

Following from this, the youngster's chances of release by the courts from security appear similarly bleak, since researchers report (DoH 1990):

> We have been surprised at the extent to which social workers' comments to the effect that 'treatment programmes take a year' have been accepted by solicitors and courts alike .... The consequence of this arrangement has been the better the youngster has done, the stronger the argument for keeping him or her in conditions of security even longer.

The 1970s saw growing pressure for reform in favour of controlling admissions to security and curbing local authority powers to lock youngsters up without reference to anyone else. It was this absolute power and the accompanying total absence of accountability that led to threats to present the issue of secure accommodation to the European Court of Human Rights. The introduction of legal criteria and court process forestalled this as these *apparently* provided the checks on local authority powers that the lobbyists sought. However, the legal criteria are relatively vague and within most local authority care systems a not insignificant percentage of the young people in care may, at some time, formally meet the criteria for security. Working as they do with sometimes quite damaged and disordered young people, who may also exhibit difficult and defiant behaviour, it is to be expected that there will be a reservoir of potential candidates for security within most care systems. This fact has not gone unnoticed by government departments, who in recognition of the potentially large group to whom the criteria *could* be applied state (DHSS 1986):

> In particular, there should not be a presumption that, because a child meets the criteria set out in the legislation, placement in security is automatically appropriate.

Studies have suggested a high level of acceptance of social work recommendations by juvenile courts. It is not surprising, therefore, that legislation with relatively indefinite criteria should result in the courts 'processing' cases with comparatively little challenge. The problem is that this can then leave the process largely dominated by the views of social services departments, who, as we have already seen, have a tendency to use the secure system as an adjunct to their own, sometimes barely adequate, resources. It remains the prerogative of the carers to select out youngsters presenting the greatest difficulties from within a larger group, all of whom could potentially satisfy the legal criteria. With the court's endorsement they may therefore be identified as candidates for secure containment on the questionable basis that their main problem is that they do not fit into what is available. There is disturbing evidence of this in the fact that currently, short-term admissions to security from the child care system account for almost one third of the total number of admissions. The predisposition for security to be used in this way continues to be the source of debate about its misuse, for at a recent conference on secure accommodation, it was reported (Allen and Hill 1990):

> There was ... concern about particular children's homes using secure care as a 'punishment block', a place where youngsters are sent to 'cool off' if they disrupt or abscond from open units.

Such injustice is made all the more perverse because of the geographical 'accident' by which it occurs. The, by now already well-documented, phenomenon of 'justice by geography' is again apparent here, since it is the 'accident' of where you live as a youngster in care, what is available there and what policies are applied, that could well decide whether you stay out or go inside. In recognition of this, there is now a growing emphasis by government on the need for local authorities to be their own censors. A gradual acknowledgement of the ineffectiveness of the legal 'controls' has led to the identification of the local authority as the focal point for the exercise of control over admissions. The question remains, however, about conflicting interests and whether local authorities can realistically be expected to exercise systemic intervention at key points in these decision-making processes when they are themselves often so directly interested in those very processes and their outcomes.

The recipients of secure containment

Studies of the kinds of youngsters placed in secure units endorse a view of them as places for 'deviants' from the care system (Millham 1978):

> Admission to security depends on making a sufficiently cogent case, a brief which relies almost entirely on a candidate's inconvenient

behaviour in other residential institutions .... At the moment it seems that the demand for security reflects the requirements of inadequate open institutions and community services rather than the needs of difficult children.

The overall picture to emerge from studies of the young people placed in secure units is one in which the numbers of disobedient and disruptive youngsters from the care system significantly surpass those who might have more cause to be termed 'dangerous' or 'a danger to themselves'. Indeed Cawson and Martell (1979) observed that of over 400 children admitted to secure units:

> [There were] only 34 who were admitted to care following offences against the person, robbery or rape and 12 following arson offences. These offences were by no means all at such a level as to create a serious risk to the life or safety of others .... In some cases the children had committed no other offences and were acting within the setting of intense relationships or family problems.

In the case of violent behaviour, the evidence suggests that, for the most part, youngsters in security who have committed violent acts have done so in the context of close personal relationships and with residential carers. Revealingly, Millham's study showed that in over two thirds of those instances involving violence towards residential staff 'the staff had quite clearly provoked violence and were the ones who hit first'. Risk to the general public from those who go into security would therefore appear to be limited to (Cawson 1986):

> ... a very small proportion of violent offenders and from children who light fires or drive stolen cars.

Indeed, the nuisance value of 'taking and driving away' is reflected in secure admissions, with almost one fifth of youngsters admitted having been convicted of this offence. Whether security could really be expected to do much to change these youngsters' behaviour patterns has been the subject of speculation, all the more so because at the same time admission to security carries with it great risks that the criminal/institutional containment it offers will serve to endorse those very patterns of behaviour it seeks to change. Hence, Cawson (1986) observed:

> It became clear that the units could not do more for offenders than contain them for a while, and that they might be criminogenic for some naive children open to the influence of more sophisticated companions.

Amongst defiant and difficult youngsters from the care system absconders and others who engaged in offending are mixed together with remanded offenders held in security sometimes on quite serious charges. Of course, supporters of the system will always argue that things have changed and *now* secure units only contain those dangerous and damaged youngsters that they 'should', but there is reason to be sceptical if this is truly the case. While the number of boys in security who have been remanded is increasing because the government policy to try and avoid remands in custody is shifting offenders across to be held in secure units, for the girls in security there seems little change. One author (Lathaen 1984) summarised his impressions after looking to see what changes might have occurred after the introduction of the courts' oversight of admissions by concluding:

> From reading through the files ... my opinion is that there has been little change in the type of child being sent to secure accommodation, whether one measures the characteristics of the child in terms of family background, type of crime committed, levels of delinquency or absconding rates.

Of clients sent from the care systems to security many, it is argued, are not as disordered or dangerous as such referral might imply. As we have seen, there is also a potentially quite large reservoir, in terms of the criteria for security, of young people in care who *could* be put forward for containment. So what is it that distinguishes those who go forward to security from those who do not? In discussing cases it is clear that there are a number of features which invariably accompany those referred to security, as follows:

1. Flagrancy

Many youngsters in care sometimes behave in dangerous and disturbing ways. This is not surprising given the evidence in Chapter 3 of this book that the majority of them may be abuse survivors. Accordingly, in any one year it is not uncommon for local authority residential units, particularly those in the inner cities, to see incidents like overdoses, wrist and body cutting, assaults, substance abuse and prostitution. Such behaviour could be linked with absconding or 'significant risk' under the formal criteria and used to justify a referral to security, but clearly this does not happen in all cases. This may be explained in terms of the 'visibility' of the damaging behaviour. Some young people engage in potentially self destructive activities in a relatively covert way and this can create an illusion that it is somehow 'under control' and is less of a problem.

Flagrant behaviour, on the other hand, soon becomes 'something-about-which-something-must-be-seen-to-be-done'. Social workers ignore flagrant behaviour at their peril. Social work staff often endeavour to contain their anxieties while working with distressed youngsters who are at risk, but are sometimes forced to weigh up risk-taking against the need to 'cover' themselves. Flagrant behaviour makes risk-taking more difficult because it opens workers to charges of irresponsibility. Worrying behaviour which does not 'advertise' itself can be more often worked with in an open setting, whereas flagrant behaviour makes this more difficult.

2. 'Uncontrollability'

This is usually taken to refer to disruptiveness in the existing, or previous, placements. Violence may be an important element here, combining with an overall felt inability by staff to 'engage' the young person. One or more 'serious incidents' in the residential unit where the youngster is placed are usually the final stage before discussion about containment is started. This scenario is clearly identified by the research. Residential staff feel defeated and abused by this time and concern is often expressed about the impact of the youngster's behaviour on other residents. What may further distinguish the candidate for security from other disruptive young people is the element of *defiance* and an apparent disregard for authority with a refusal to accept control. As a result, respect for the 'standing' of the unit is felt by staff to have been undermined. A powerful lobby can develop, with workers demanding the removal of the youngster and it is not unusual for this to be accompanied by threats of industrial action. Despite research evidence that it is probably better to move youngsters on from placements that have become 'redundant' to a different, open placement, the 'push' created by the series of events in the residential unit can move the client towards security instead.

3. Absence of an alternative placement

This has by now become something of a major issue, given the shortage of alternative open provision in most care systems. Probably because of this the government's Guidance and Regulations for secure accommodation under the Children's Act makes certain to emphasise that this should not be a reason for resorting to security (DoH 1990):

> Placement in a secure unit must be a 'last resort' in the sense that all else must first have been comprehensively considered and rejected — never because no other placement was available at the relevant time ....

The besieged residential service manager, meanwhile, under pressure from workers wanting the youngster removed, looks for another open unit and finds none that will accept. Lack of a range of resources in open units leaves staff feeling unqualified to take on what are rightly seen as difficult cases. The residential manager, pushed for time to effect the transfer, finds a secure place and that is that. 'Service considerations' find a meeting ground with the youngster's behaviour, with a secure admission as the result. Necessity becomes the mother of invention.

The decision makers

It is in relation to the rest of the service that the youngster's behavioural difficulties are thrown into sharpest relief. An interplay begins between the objective behaviour of the young person and a range of other 'considerations' brought into the decision-making process by carers and managers. As the drama unfolds the various actors come to centre-stage to speak their lines. There are no villains in this play, only the tendency of staff to represent the different areas of concern as they affect their colleagues', and their own, fields of responsibility.

The residential faction is commonly most acutely conscious of disruption to the care system, with unit staff concern focused usually at the local level and service managers mindful of the need to keep the whole organisation operational. The apparent hopelessness experienced by staff in the light of persistent, difficult behaviour in the domestic/residential setting often unites with the consideration of *risk*. As carriers of the statutory case responsibility, it is invariably fieldwork staff who, understandably, spearhead this debate. Assessment of the degree of risk to which a youngster is felt to be exposed is of course usually a matter of some contention and opinions can vary considerably among professionals. It is only very recently that 'risk' has been (partially) addressed by the Children Act Guidance and Regulations on Secure Accommodation, which stipulates that the young person must be thought likely to suffer 'significant' harm. While still open to interpretation, this specification may help the sometimes acrimonious discussion over risk that can occur as different social services staff get drawn into the pressured discourse about what to do next.

Policy considerations might also insert themselves into the process of debate. In terms of policies towards secure accommodation, local authorities appear to be a 'broad church', as the recent DoH Working Party report pointed out (DoH 1989):

> For some authorities locking up children, and hence the provision of secure facilities themselves, is politically unacceptable. In others, there are varying degrees of professional ambivalence .... Against this, there are a number of local authorities who are substantial users of secure accommodation.

The mother of invention 83

A 'whirlpool effect' can develop as the different parties jostle to get their view expressed and this can cause decisions to be made erratically, and the process of decision-making itself may well be confused. While the DoH makes reference to political 'intrusion' into decisions on use of secure accommodation as an issue (and this clearly does have a great impact on patterns of usage) it nevertheless puts its faith in the need to make decisions about using security at a high *management* level within social services departments. With the courts' intervention making little impact, the hope is that the authorities can become their own gatekeepers. Hence (DoH 1990):

> ... local authorities have the major role to play in ensuring that the policy objectives at the pre-admission stage are met (what we shall term the 'gatekeeping role).

Accordingly, the DoH's recommended form of gatekeeping is that (DoH 1990):

> Each local authority should designate a senior officer (preferably at Director or Assistant Director level) to act as a 'gatekeeper' for all requests to place a child in the authority's care in secure accommodation ... ensuring that the statutory criteria were met; that no other alternative form of dealing with the case was appropriate, and that the placement was able to meet the needs of the child.

While of course it is desirable to review all the areas listed above, it must be questionable whether allocating these tasks to a senior social services manager will realistically alter patterns of usage of security. The need for better co-ordination in local authorities around young people admitted into secure units is clear, and to this extent the identification of a 'gatekeeper' may help. However, whether they could be expected to resist the pressures outlined previously — pressures often arising more from the problems of managing *services* than clients — is open to question.

What is going on?

Although there are proposals to improve research and monitor secure accommodation usage in some regions, it is still difficult to get a clear picture of what practices and controls are being applied in local authorities. Three authorities were therefore contacted and asked to be interviewed about their own use of secure units. All agreed, with two requesting anonymity. In line with government emphasis on senior management oversight and control of secure accommodation usage, the respective assistant directors were contacted and asked whether they would like to be interviewed. Alternatively, they could nominate another member of staff who was more directly involved with secure unit usage than themselves. On being invited to do this, all nominated third tier officers. It was immediately apparent that the government emphasis on senior management oversight has not found a meeting ground with operational imperatives, and that it is middle management who are effectively the main brokers in their local systems as they relate to security.

Of the three authorities selected, 'Red' has been under Labour administration for many years and is recognised as 'politically radical'. 'White' has been under Labour since 1986 and is more moderate politically. 'Blue' is a staunch Conservative borough. All of the authorities have social services departments which are organised both functionally and geographically (i.e. with specialist borough-wide services for children as well as with district or area-based services). Interestingly, all of the principal officers nominated for interview as 'lead figures' in the department over security worked for specialist, borough-wide services.

The statistics for their respective care populations are as shown in Table 5.1.

Table 5.1

Authority	Total children in care	Children in care per 1000 population	Percentage boarded out	Percentage in community home	Other
Red	810	14.95	58	20	22
White	404	13.88	45	24	31
Blue	260	8.93	63	18	19

Each representative was shown the Regional Planning Authority figures indicating their secure placements made over the last two years which, notably, bore no consistent statistical relationship to the number of children in care across the authorities. White emerged as a high user and the interviewee expressed surprise at this at first, but soon deduced that this was due to repeated short-term admissions — a worrying pattern in some authorities. None of those interviewed were familiar with the figures and knew of no mechanism whereby the annual regional statistics were presented for the consideration of managers or politicians.

When considering the figures showing trends in the use of security in their own boroughs, and comparisons with the other authorities, there were some interesting responses. Red's inter- viewee immediately queried the inferences that might be drawn from the statistics.

> What you've got to appreciate is that numbers of placements don't in any way reflect the number of kids who are at risk. In this authority political pressure has resulted in a decline in the number of place- ments made, yet over the same period there's good reason to believe

The mother of invention 85

that real circumstances for people are worse. Ultimately one would expect there to be a connection between the level of deprivation locally, and the disorder that it produces, and secure accommodation usage; but it just isn't simple because many other variables intervene.

While in Red authority the trends had mainly been affected by political intervention, the other two authorities identified service developments as the main influence. Both cited the development of specialist services as a major factor, for, as White said:

> The creation of our Children's Division has created a better range of services for adolescents. Also, there is a focussed body of people to scrutinise and question poor professional practice, and we expect this to reduce admissions to secure accommodation.

All three authorities could point to superficial evidence that usage had declined. The impact of political intervention is not surprising, nor is the availability of more services. The lobby of 'specialist practitioners' is an interesting area and many indicate that attitudinal change, perhaps spearheaded by staff with a special commitment to the 'secure unit client group', could have as important an impact as these other factors. In that sense, the creation of functional specialisation may well be beneficial to the quality of youth social work in social services departments.

No authority had a system for recording and collating information on clients and secure accommodation as such, the main source of information being individual client's files. Only Red had a partial record of requests for security in the form of the records of its Secure Accommodation Sub-Committee, to which all cases are required to be presented for members' consideration. These records, however, are not periodically collated to produce an overview. None of the authorities produce summary reports on the number and character of admissions and only Blue has an annual report to the Social Services Committee — on long-term secure placements of which over the last few years there have been none.

The absence of any summary reports was surprising given that all the interviewees reported a strong critical interest in secure accommodation within their authorities. One consistent reason for this lack of overview was because there was no 'product champion' for secure accommodation to monitor the Department's activities and it is here that the DoH suggestion for such a role to be established can be seen to be a good one. Within departments, responsibilities for the oversight of secure accommodation usage often seems to fall between a number of stools. The lack of monitoring also extended to instances where security had come under *consideration*, but not been pursued. Only Blue authority had a procedure for secure accommodation case conferences, but the outcomes from these were not collated such that the number of children who come under consideration for security is known. Similiarly, no authority kept records of instances when a secure placement was sought but no placement made because none was available. One respondent spoke for all, saying:

> This is the biggest inhibition now on secure placement. There are many occasions when we look for a place but can't get one. Sometimes there's one in somewhere like Liverpool, and that's not on so we give up.

Limitation on availability is clearly in turn limiting usage and this might indicate that further contraction of provision could be promoted as a response to this in preference to further expansion. This was brought home when the authorities were asked what actually happened to clients in those instances where no resource was available. All authorities described situations where the 'high profile' response of secure accommodation is, of necessity, then replaced by a much more arms-length intervention. The interviewee in Blue authority said.

> We have had a number of cases when clients can't go into secure units. We can't contain them in our own services so we usually place them in bedsits. We then try to allocate a lot of staff time towards supporting them. They invariably have some trouble but, surprisingly, most make out OK eventually.

The authorities echoed similar descriptions whereby the removal of the young person from the point of conflict, usually the care system, provided a solution. Understandably, this left considerable anxiety, and some 'worrying' episodes were reported, but only one instance was outlined when the youngster was re-referred for containment.

For those who are placed in security there is a disturbing absence of clear procedures to ensure their prompt removal. While some attention has been given to the issue of admission, discharge is largely left to social workers to determine, unless the stay becomes a long one and attracts the attention of more senior staff or politicians. It is also important to note that no authority has systems for monitoring remands into custody. This is an interesting area, for an authority's low use of secure accommodation may not necessarily indicate good practice if there is a relatively high number of young people remanded into custody. However, while all the authorities regarded the decisions around remands into custody similarly seriously (but again without expressing this in clear procedures), there was no facility to record these decisions and compare performance here against secure usage. Additionally, Red and White authorities reported members' ambivalence about the use of security as an alternative to 'certificates of unruliness', with only a reluctant acceptance of closed units being used as an alternative in this way.

Only in Red authority were instances reported where the decision-maker, the sub-Committee, had refused to agree to secure placements. In the other authorities, where the decision is made at officer (formally Assistant Director) level, recommendations are mandated. There is of course no reason why any one authority should generate more applications that are turned down by the 'gatekeeper' than another. Indeed, one might expect even more thoroughly-prepared applications when they are required to be presented for members' consideration. It would appear, therefore, that the politically-led sub-committee in Red authority, with its highly critical attitude towards secure accommodation, is able to resist the pressure to make placements in a way that senior social services officers are not.

Members are relatively removed from the management of the care system and perhaps less mindful of the consequences of refusal to admit in terms of the difficulties this can leave for case and service managers alike. This may indicate the need to reconsider the DoH suggestion that senior officers act as gatekeepers to security against the desirability of corporate devices for making decisions, involving parties not directly involved in the management of the services within which the young people are placed. To some extent what the interviews identified was the impact of *politics* in service delivery. In Red authority the intrusion of political ideology is apparent and its effect on the usage of secure accommodation pervasive. In White authority political pressure is tangential rather than direct, but still informs officers' responses. In all the authorities one can see that 'admissions figures' tell us nothing about the problems of clients in the care system. Political, ideological and managerial factors obfuscate any one-to-one relationship between client need and secure accommodation placements.

The poor information systems within all the authorities make it difficult for them to adopt a strategic rather than reactive approach to the use of secure provision. There is evidence of ideological 'window dressing' in terms of critiques of secure provision, but little clear strategy is set in relation to its use. It may be that the functional/geographic split in these authorities has some impact on the fact that no-one seemed to 'own' the issue. It falls between the statutory case carriers (geographic staff) and the service managers (functional staff). Departments would benefit from clearly identifying responsibility for secure accommodation — not just for the *process* but also for the *issue*.

As expected, the study indicated that courts are a relatively unimportant part of the process. However, the court system may be helping to reduce the number of long-stay placements in security. The 'impressionistic' evidence gathered by the study indicated that, as in the earlier studies of the 1970s, secure accommodation usage is largely about 'control' issues of difficult and defiant clients in the care system. It is worrying that this seems to be continuing, but there can be little doubt that secure provision will continue to be used by pressured residential systems for as long as it is available to them. The formal controls simply are not adequate to prevent usage of security for this purpose.

Guidelines on decision-making in this area are clearly needed. The DoH could arguably do more to assist politicians and officers alike. A clearer system of Secure Accommodation Conferences within the authorities could help considerably. Such a system would encourage 'networking' to look at alternatives and clarify explicitly the bases upon which a decision is made, or recommendation put forward.

Finally, the issue concerning the availability of secure provision raises some disturbing questions. Avilability appears as a major factor determining the local authority's usage. However, following from the failure to obtain placements, it is illuminating that 'collapse' does not seem to happen to those clients left, by default, in the community. Rather, as Chapter 6 of this book indicates, an intensive but low-profile approach seems to work just as well with them.

Conclusions — abolition of evolution?

Most social work practitioners will concede that some very disturbed clients do need to be contained. The problem with the institutions that provide the containment is their tendency to draw in inappropriate populations. The old maxim 'if the institutions are there, they will be used' rings as true of secure accommodation as of other lock-ups and begs the questions of whether these tendencies towards misuse dictate that we should simply close the units down. It is questions of this sort that have led others to the conclusion that the inappropriate incarceration of groups of people is an inevitable corollary to institutional containment. In the so-called 'Massachusetts Experiment' in America, large numbers of young people were simply released from penal institutions. This offered graphic evidence that to close institutions is in fact the best way to reduce their populations. With many young people already being put forward for secure accommodation, but not being placed through lack of available places, one is left to wonder what would happen if the facility to contain youngsters was withdrawn altogether. There is evidence to suggest, as in Massachusetts, that other facilities could as readily help those that need it without locking them away.

The problem for those advocating abolition is that proponents of containment always cite an extreme case to illustrate the need for the whole system, and ask 'what do you propose to put in its place?'. However, the abolitionist perspective considers first and foremost the abusive nature of institutions and seeks their removal for their negative and dangerous impact on people's lives. The social activist Mathieson (1974) draws attention to this when he talks of the 'expelled' as that group of people Western society routinely strips of social status and often legal and civil rights in the process of incarcerating them. He urges us not to be drawn into constructing alternative ways of dealing with institutional populations but, as in Massachusetts, to simply abolish the institutions.

Cohen (1976) proposes a more 'gradualist' strategy, arguing that for abolitionism to succeed it would need to contain three major components:

1. a total moratorium on the construction of new institutions;
2. decarceration of all who can be safely released;
3. excarceration, by stopping admissions to establishments by severely limiting the *powers* to make admissions.

It is interesting to note that during the history of secure accommodation the sensitive and controversial nature of its existence has led all three of these strategies to be considered. In relation to the first strategy, research evidence showing that secure units were filling up with 'light end' young people eventually created enough misgivings to stop the proliferation of units and their numbers have now decreased. However, this may change again as pressure mounts to prevent youngsters from being remanded into custody and placed instead in secure units. This might well produce the 'need' for more places and we may see the range of provision increasing again. For some, this is reckoned to be a good thing as it allows the abolition of prison department custody for juvenile offenders (Allen and Hill 1990):

> After abolition, secure units will play a small but important role in the criminal justice landscape, certainly not as replacements for custody, but as placements of the last resort for those few juvenile offenders from whom the public need protection and the even smaller number who have committed the most serious offences and may require protection themselves.

While such optimism might seem incautious in the light of the history of secure accommodation, perhaps the authors are right to place their faith in secure units becoming solely an adjunct to the penal system. Security has traditionally occupied a unique and ambivalent midpoint on the treatment–punishment continuum. This has led to the well-documented bizarre admixture of young people in occupation and the concomitant confusion over the purpose of secure units. To resolve the dilemma in favour of linking security directly to custody would at least have the advantage of preventing its use as a dustbin for the care system, were it to be done.

Cohen's second strategy involves releasing those who can safely be released. To a limited extent one can see this having been encouraged through the legislation that now requires local authorities to remove youngsters from units at the earliest possible time. However, 'drift' appears indigenous to the care system and secure accommodation is no exception to the rule. Local authorities clearly could do a lot more to exercise their responsibility to remove young people promptly and there is disappointingly little apparent committment to establishing fail-safe systems to ensure youngsters do not linger in secure units. One suspects that it is the lack of available alternatives that is the bugbear here. It has been suggested that secure admissions are related to (limited) provision in local authorities and by the same token so must be secure accommodation discharges. The resource implications here are obvious and to be successful in the current climate social services staff will need to press hard for the necessary open units. However, what is needed may not be that much and the potential may already exist within existing resources, as is discussed in Chapter 6 of this book. Nevertheless, local authorities must find better ways to provide the intensive help needed for young people in crisis if they are to avoid using the closed units.

Finally, Cohen suggested the strategy of 'excarceration' — not sending people into institutions in the first place by constructing rigorous 'gates' at the points of entry. This strategy would seem to hold considerable potential and clearly local authorities could, as some have, construct policies and practices that would severely limit the use of security and eradicate, if that is possible, its misuse. With the failure of legal process via the courts to achieve this, the ball has moved back into the court of the local authority in this respect.

By the 1990s the impact of systems management on social work with young people is obvious and there is already considerable experience of applying these methods to control the movement of youngsters into appropriate rather than damaging provision. With government now putting its faith in the local authorities to develop better controls at local level, the time therefore has now come for those social services departments that have not yet done so to apply a systematic schema to the 'field of operations' surrounding secure accommodation. Some scepticism must remain that controlling access better will merely serve to slightly alter the groups of young people put forward for security, but for the time being, it is the best strategy to explore and exploit.

References

Allen R, Hill G 1990 Placements of the last resort. *Community Care* 15 November

Cawson P 1986 *Long term Secure Accommodation: A Review of Evidence and Discussion of London's Need.* LBCRPC

Cawson P, Martell M 1979 *Children Referred to Closed Units.* DHSS Research Report No. 5, HMSO

Cohen S 1979 *How do we balance guilt, justice and tolerance.* RAP

Department of Health 1989 *Report of the Secure Accommodation Working Party*

Department of Health 1990 *Children Act 1989 — Consultation Paper No. 1, Secure Accommodation (Guidance and Regulations)*

Holden A 1985 *Children in Care.* Comyn Books

Lathaen A 1984 *Secure Accommodation in London.* LBCRP

Mathiesen T 1974 *The Politics of Abolition.* Marvin Robertson

Millham S 1978 *Locking Up Children.* Saxon House

6 The hard core — taking young people out of secure institutions

Cathy Aymer, Joan Gittens, Dave Hill, Ian McLeod, John Pitts, Marica Rytovaata, Eileen Sturdivant, Larry Wright and Marietta Walker

> This chapter considers the predicament of a small group of young people who, despite central and local government policies aimed at taking youngsters out of closed institutions, or preventing them from entering them in the first place are, nonetheless, consigned to them. It explores who they are, how they got there and how they might be released.

In recent years the numbers of young people entering custody and secure accommodation in the local authority where the study reported in this chapter was undertaken has dropped substantially. As a result of strict monitoring and gatekeeping, in the two years to the end of December 1989, only 19 juveniles entered a detention centre, a youth custody centre/young offenders institution, a secure unit or a youth treatment centre. If we add those young people who were in the care system, aged over 17, and sentenced to custody in adult courts, this figure rises to 28 but this is still a very small number.

Targetting
Many local authorities have achieved similar reductions in the past decade but it would be a mistake to assume, as some commentators have, that such reductions indicate that agents of local care and juvenile justice systems are necessarily making more rational decisions or targetting their interventions more accurately. In his study Parker [1989, p118] observed that:

> there is no straightforward relationship between the seriousness of the offences and custody potential. The results in Yellowtown and Redtown are particularly 'shapeless', the seriousness of offending seemed to have an almost random effect on the way the magistrates regarded the cases in relation to custody.

Such discrepancies were evident in the juvenile court which dealt with most of the juvenile offenders in our study. Whereas one bench sentenced a young man with two counts of theft to the detention centre for 21 days, another sentenced one charged with the same number of similar offences to youth custody for six months. As to violent offences; one young man found guilty of robbery received four months youth custody while another received six weeks in a detention centre.

The irrationality of custodial sentencing echoes the observations of Millham (1978) and Dennington (this volume), that decisions to place young people in secure accommodation are far more closely related to the willingness of an approved school or children's home to deal with them than the objective problems they presented. As a consequence some institutions made frequent use of secure accommodation while others made none. Dennington [in Chapter 5 of this book] indicates that it is not necessarily the 'hard core' of dangerous and self-damaging children and young people, those for whom secure accommodation was designed, who go into security or custody but those who test out an overstretched staff team, fail to conform to institutional rules or just do not 'fit in' anywhere else. This was also our finding and it adds up to poor targetting and begs questions about who is being locked up and why?

Routes to 'security' and custody

The idea of a 'system career' presumes that people's identities may be spoiled by internalising deviant labels imposed upon them by powerful 'agents of control' (Becker 1963, Goffman 1968). This may have the effect of propelling them into a deviant career in which they are forced into association with people who have been similarly labelled. These social groups, often institutional populations, then attract even greater attention from agents of control and this serves to amplify their deviance and to further damage their already spoiled identities.

A system career describes the route a person who has been labelled in this way follows through administrative and judicial processes and social institutions. In the studies of the careers of young people in the juvenile justice system undertaken at Lancaster University we are presented with a model of a system career in which a young person, once inserted in the system, escalates through a tariff of penalties which culminates in imprisonment (Thorpe et al. 1980). There is no reason to believe that this is not an accurate depiction of many juvenile justice system careers in the 1970s and early 1980s when far larger numbers of young people were entering the juvenile justice system.

In 1973 over 7000 children and young people were living in approved schools, yet by 1983 under 2000 were placed in their post-1969 Act equivalent, community homes (with education) (CHE). The reduction in CHE placements was, in large part, a result of closures by local authorities who, faced with substantial cutbacks in public expenditure, opted for adolescent fostering and intensive intermediate treatment as a cost effective alternative (Personal Social Services Council 1979, Thorpe et al. 1980, Curtis 1989). This trend was bolstered by a growing recognition of the tendency of the residential 'solution' to generate its own peculiar, and sometimes intractable, problems (Millham et al. 1975).

The decline in the number of CHE places was accompanied initially by an increase in the use of custody. It appears that the juvenile bench, having been effectively deprived of the approved school/CHE as a sentencing option, compensated, by imposing a greater number of custodial sentences (Farrington 1985). While this explanation accounts for the rise in the number of juveniles receiving custodial sentences from 6900 in 1977 to 7900 in 1981, the heyday of CHE closures, it does not explain the subsequent dramatic fall in the use of custody. By 1989 the numbers of custodial sentences imposed on juveniles in England and Wales had dropped to around 2000. This decline is attributable in part to a 10 per cent decrease in the number of teenagers in the population but it is largely due to changes in the ways agents of the juvenile justice system dealt young offenders.

The growth of police cautioning and the development of interagency panels had the effect of diverting substantial numbers of young people from court. Nationally, the proportion of males aged between 14 and 16 who were cautioned rose from 34 per cent in 1980 to 58 per cent in 1987. For females, cautions increased from 58 per cent to 82 per cent in the same period. In some areas precourt diversion was so successful in keeping young people out of court that they were declared 'custody-free zones' (Rutherford 1986).

An important contribution to the decline of juvenile incarceration in the 1980s was made by alternatives to custody projects, many of which were developed as part of the DHSS 'new initiative' in intermediate treatment launched in 1983 (NACRO 1988). Where new initiative projects operated, there is clear evidence of significant reductions in the use of custodial sentencing by magistrates.

Taken together, these developments have meant that by the late 1980s far fewer system careers were ending in confinement in a secure unit or custody. Possibly as a result of this, rather than the linear escalation of system careers described by Thorpe (1980), the careers of the young people we studied often looked more like a pinball machine in overdrive. One boy had had 74 placements or referrals in the preceeding three years, moving rapidly between local authority care, the juvenile justice system, special education and adolescent psychiatric facilities. Denne (1990) writes:

> when juvenile justice workers first became successful in diverting children from custody there was evidence that receptions into care rose ... it may be that the maintenance of more children at home in one system exerts sufficient pressure on others to increase the flow there.

Sometimes referrals were wholly appropriate; rational responses to real problems. Others were pragmatic, as in the case of the educationally handicapped young person whom teachers and social workers believed was being sexually abused by his father, who was referred to a residential school. Referrals between systems also served as a solution to the problems those systems were experiencing in managing young people. Sometimes, when staff in a clinic, project or children's home had exhausted all available sanctions, referral sideways was used as an alternative to referral to secure accomodation or a telephone call to the police. This said, it was not the case that young people entered these systems arbitrarily.

It appeared that insertion into systems was determined as much by the social class, race and gender of the young person as the 'problems' they were experiencing.

Class, race, gender and system careers

It is clear that the young people who entered secure accommodation presented considerable problems to the adults who had responsibility for them. It is less clear, however, whether at earlier stages of their system careers, and in some cases at the point of referral to security, they presented qualitatively different problems, in terms of their behaviour, than many of the patients admitted to, or registered as outpatients with, the local, non-secure, regional adolescent psychiatric unit.

A comparison of the young people entering security and those admitted to, or attending, the unit serves as an interesting example of the impact that class, race and gender may have on the referral, placement and modes of treatment offered to troublesome young people. The following extracts from case notes describe young people who were referred to secure accommodation.

— Mood swings; from co-operativeness to abuse and violence.
— ... alternates between co-operative and disruptive, in a verbal and physical way.

— ... becomes sullen and abusive, verbally and physically.
— We are unable to contain him.
— ... finds it hard to express his feelings in positive or constructive ways ...

These descriptions of behaviour, written by workers in open residential establishments about young people they wished to transfer to secure accomodation, are remarkably similar to statements made by GPs and psychiatrists wishing to refer patients suffering from 'conduct' and 'emotional' disorders, to adolescent psychiatric facilities. Although the unit deals with a broader range of problems, the differences between the referrals to secure accommodation and referrals to the unit could not be accounted for simply in terms of differences in the behaviour of the young people so referred.

This raises the question of whether it is the significance attributed to problematic behaviour rather than the behaviour itself which determines the system into which a young person will be inserted. 18 of the 28 young people in our study had spent substantial periods of their lives in residential care. All of them had had a social worker at some point; some for most of their lives. All had been referred to secure accommodation by social workers. One had been referred to an adolescent psychiatric unit. Of the 90 children and young people referred to the unit in 1988/9, 9 had been referred by their GPs, 46 by psychiatrists 4 by the education service and 28 by local authority social workers.

In discussion with staff of the local authority assessment service and the unit it became apparent that social class, race and gender played a significant part in determining the point of referral, the system into which young people were inserted and their subsequent system careers. The more prosperous parents also tended to be white and they were unlikely to take their problems to the social services department. They would, instead, tend to consult their GP. The GP would in turn tend to refer them on to a psychiatrist in the local hospital since psychiatry is the branch of medicine which deals with behaviour and emotions. The psychiatrist would then, if she or he deemed it appropriate, refer them on to the unit. Thus the young person, once inserted into a medical/psychiatric system would become a medical/psychiatric problem and they would become a patient. The patient would then embark upon a medical/psychiatric career. 16.6 per cent of patients discharged from the unit in the three years prior to June 1988 were subsequently admitted to a psychiatric institution. None were admitted to a prison.

The young people who entered secure accommodation by contrast, were, almost without exception, drawn from deprived working class families. Having a social worker and being in care are things which tend to happen only to the poorest people in our society and located within this group are a disproportionately large number of black people. Once inserted into the system their careers run along familiar pathways, developing a peculiar logic and momentum, not least because the solution to the persistent breakdown of the institutional solution is, almost always, further institutionalisation.

Far more young women were admitted to the adolescent psychiatric unit than to security or custody. It seemed that one reason for the larger number of female referrals to the unit is the tendency of young women to internalise their problems in the form of depression and self damage, rather than act them out in ways which are threatening or challenging to adults. They present a problem of adjustment rather than containment and to that extent come to be regarded as suitable cases for 'treatment'. Only when young women externalise and act out their problems in the form of flagrant 'promiscuity' or violence are they seen to present problems of containment and they then become suitable candidates for secure accommodation (Gelsthorpe 1983). Of the 31 patients discharged from the unit in the three years to June 1988 20 were male and 11 were female. In 1988 and 1989 only one young woman entered security or custody.

While in general we might expect young men to externalise or act out problems and young women to internalise them it is also the case that middle class and working class young men tend to 'act out' problems in substantially different ways which are culturally prescribed and determined by access to opportunity. As a result, the ways in which middle class young men act out tends to be perceived as less threatening or challenging by adults (Cicourel 1968).

There is a growing body of evidence that black young people are perceived by adult professionals in the educational, psychiatric, justice and welfare fields as the most threatening group of all and they are, as a result, far more prone to containment and far less likely to be offered less restrictive options (Pitts 1986, 1988). Over 80 per cent of the juveniles sentenced to custody and over 60 per cent of those placed in secure accommodation in the study period were black or non-British nationals. By contrast, black young people constituted only 6.4 per cent of patients discharged from the unit during the period.

This over-representation is more stark when set against contemporary data on the racial make-up of the area which indicates that white British people constituted 60.5 per cent of the population, black British/Afro-Carribean people 4 per cent and Morrocan and Turkish people, taken together, something liked 0.003 per cent. On this basis, around one third as many white British juveniles (3) as might have been expected were sentenced to custody, 16 times as many black British/Afro-Carribean juveniles (8), and around 2000 times as many Morrocan and Turkish Juveniles (3).

Obviously the number of young people involved is very small and any inferences about the meaning of this data must be made with great caution. Yet the inescapable implication is that during the two-year period of our study poor, black, or non-British young men were at far greater risk of losing their liberty than their white counterparts.

These were young people who had usually passed through a series of institutions in different systems on their routes to custody and security. It is to the ways in which the staff of these institutions make their assessments of such young people, assessments which will have a profound effect on their system careers, that we now turn.

Assessment

On reading reports and child-care reviews which offered assessments of young people referred to secure accommodation we noted that comments tended to concentrate on observed behaviour, making little reference to significant events which might have affected that behaviour. It would appear, for example, that absconding frequently followed a visit from family members, a home visit or the commission of a criminal offence, but in the assessments such absconding tended to be explained in terms of the young person's psychological or emotional predisposition. There was little or no information on the nature of the placements which 'broke down' and precipitated the referral to security. There was no mention of the number of other young people and staffing levels in the establishment, levels of tension and conflict, and the techniques and philosophy adopted by the residential establishment. There was also no mention of the chain of events which precipitated the behaviour which led to the referral to secure accommodation.

The assessments we read tended to locate the origins of the problematic situations in which these young people played a central role within the young people themselves rather than the networks of which they were part. As such they ran the risk of perpetrating what psychologists call the 'fundamental attribution error' in which situations which arise out of interactions between the actor and her or his environment are wrongly perceived as an expression of their intrinsic characteristics.

The risks in this approach to assessment seemed to us to be fivefold:

The hard core

1. It does not distinguish, or trace the relationship, between the stresses and strains in the residential establishment or foster placement and the difficulties manifested by the young person.
2. It does not consider the effectiveness of the professional network, of which the residential establishment or foster placement is a part, and how it might be changed in order to contain and respond creatively to the young person.
3. It does not explore the possible impact of events in the young person's family/social network on her/his behaviour.
4. It does not explore the extent to which the difficulties might be a product of a mismatch between the needs and capabilities of the young person and the regime of the residential establishment.
5. In does not pick up behaviour which is a response to discrimination. In our study, for example, we found that four out of five of the non-habitual absconders we identified were black and had absconded from a regional facility about which concern over staff and residents racism had previously been expressed.

If we fail to distinguish between behaviour which is the property of the network and behaviour which is the property of a member of that network, we are destined to misunderstand what we see. But even if this important distinction is borne in mind and an accurate and sensitive assessment is produced, the widespread confusion about what security is and what it is supposed to do means that the impact of the assessment on the subsequent system career of the young person will be minimal.

What is security?

All too often, social workers and social work theorists use words and concepts in the same way that drunkards use lamposts; for support rather than illumination. Words which initially express concepts of great subtlety are reduced to euphemisms which present a simplified reality and obscure rather than enhance meaning.

The most notorious of these is, of course, 'community', followed closely by 'culture' and, in the wake of its transformation in the Griffith Report (1988), 'network'. Following close on their heels however is the concept of 'security'.

In practice, 'security' usually refers to what happens when all else fails, when we run out of options, when 'push comes to shove'. And one of the problems with this notion of security as the 'end of the line' is that it seems to prevent us exploring the many fruitful possibilities thrown up by the concept.

Security as protection for young people

Some of the young people who ask to be admitted, or whose behaviour leads to a referral to secure provision are very frightened of other people or themselves. Often these other people are adults and members of their own family. Whether this is a realistic fear, and as Chapter 3 of this book indicates such fear is probably both more prevalent and more realistic than we have previously been prepared to accept, it can still generate enormous anxiety for young people.

Those who are frightened of themselves may sometimes feel out of control and they may well be. They may be suffering from high levels of anxiety or feeling homicidal or suicidal. The tragic suicides of the young offenders in Armley jail, Leeds, in 1990 are a salutary reminder however that being 'locked-up' does not necessarily offer protection from self-harm. This raises the question of whether these real fears can be effectively addressed and an appropriate degree of 'security' offered in an open setting in a non-stigmatising way.

Security as a respite from anxiety for responsible adults

One of the barriers to working in this way is the respite from anxiety which secure units provide for adults who have responsibility for difficult, dangerous, seriously delinquent or self-damaging young people. To work outside a secure institution with these young people means devising an administrative structure and support systems which address the genuine concerns and anxieties of those who carry such responsibility. Such structures are discussed in detail in Chapter 8 of this book.

Security as a political strategy

Social workers may sometimes suggest a remand in secure accommodation to magistrates or judges who are contemplating remanding in custody a persistent or serious juvenile offender, or one who is likely to 'jump bail'. If a local authority is the subject of a media investigation into the profligate behaviour of adolescents in its care, as happens from time to time, there will sometimes be pressure from vocal members of the public and councillors for social workers to exert greater control through the use of secure accommodation.

Both of these situations, particularly the latter, are ones in which secure accommodation, if used, will be solving political and legal problems for politicians, magistrates and the agents of the justice system. It will solve nothing for the young people involved or their victims. The strategic use of secure accommodation, though rare, is unethical and raises the question of whether work with young people in crisis can be moved further away from the political arena.

Security as punishment

Sometimes young people in care are a terrible nuisance. They are rude to everybody, appear to appreciate nothing which is done for them and try to sabotage the best efforts of their social workers. These are the young people about whom 'vengeance reports' are sometimes written (Parker 1989). Vengeance reports are character assassinations and they tend to be written by frustrated social workers who have run out of ideas, patience and a sense of perspective. The problem is to devise a support system which feeds in new ideas or strategies, supports and helps workers who are frustrated and offers them new perspectives and approaches.

Security as an organisational safety valve

The British residential child-care system is understaffed, under-resourced and under stress. Millham (1978) notes that as early as the mid-1970s secure units were serving as an expansion tank for a system which was less and less able to respond to disturbed or difficult young people.

In our study, residential social workers have said that the capacity of their units to work effectively with some young people was largely determined by staffing levels and staff stability. When the staff team was stable they could contain very difficult youngsters and undertake creative work with them. If there was a high turnover of staff, however, young people would become less relaxed and the unit more tense. In these circumstances the most disturbed and least integrated young people became most anxious and this heightened the possibility of disruptive or violent behaviour. At this point the unit became vulnerable. It was in danger of dipping into a downward spiral which could often only be halted when the most disturbed or threatening young person was removed, sometimes for their own protection. Keeping young people out of secure accommodation it seems, is closely linked to engendering stability in mainstream residential units. This theme is developed in Chapter 4 of this book.

Security and dependency

The irony of emotional deprivation is that instead of equipping those so deprived with an enhanced capacity for independent living, it intensifies their desire for dependency while diminishing their ability to cope with the intimacy which such dependency entails. Institutions do not offer intimacy and so they are perfect for young people who fear both intimacy and freedom. But for many young people, particulary those who have spent much of their lives moving from placement to placement, freedom has little value. Pitts (1990, p. 129) writes:

> Some young people try to get caught and 'put away' because this feels better to them than 'freedom'. Saul Bellow says that we must either organise our freedom or drown in it and a lot of our young clients are in danger of drowning in it. A freedom which requires a young person to be alone in a cold flat with the dole money spent and the heat and light cut off compares unfavourably with a captivity which allows them to play pool in a warm association hall after a hot dinner.

For these young people our job is to wean them away from dependency on total institutions.

Expanding and contracting systems

Situations which result in a placement in a secure unit have a history which unfolds over time. The progression from a tolerable to an intolerable situation, although sometimes rapid, is seldom instantaneous.

The story of Michael

Background

Michael had lived with his mother from birth. She had a history of psychiatric problems and when Michael was younger she had sometimes used LSD. She was convinced that Michael was doomed because of his natural father's 'tainted genes' and because he had been 'born under the knife', he had been delivered by ceasarian section. Michael had lost contact with his real father in early childhood and his mother had subsequently had a series of partners.

Initial referral

At the age of 13 Michael was referred to an adolescent psychiatric unit by his school because of his mother's concern about conflict between Michael and his current 'stepfather'. His mother said that he was out of control and dangerous because he had threatened 'stepfather' with a knife. The unit recommended that because of the present conflict and the history of instability in the family,

Michael should be placed in a boarding school where he would receive individual therapy.

First placement breakdown
The following year Michael was suspended from his boarding school for 'sadistic and dangerous behaviour towards younger boys'. The headmaster had called the police who believed the head but could not find enough evidence to charge Michael.

Second referral
Michael, his mother and 'stepfather' appeared for a family session with two therapists and the headmaster who recounted the events which had led up to the suspension. Michael's mother became very upset and claimed that he had probably abused his younger brother and that she believed that he was working as a rent-boy in the holidays. She refused to have him back at home. On hearing this the headmaster refused to have him back at school. A social worker was called and Michael was taken into voluntary care in an open children's home.

Second placement breakdown
That same night Michael got into conflict with a member of staff. He became uncontrollable and was taken to a secure unit.

Third referral
The staff in the unit were concerned about how distressed Michael was, and that he was very threatening and sexually provocative to the other young people in the unit. A case conference was convened and attended by the field social worker whose responsibility Michael now was, the two therapists from the adolescent psychiatric unit, two staff from the secure unit and an IT worker. It was decided to place Michael in a small residential unit in his own neighbourhood where he could keep in contact with his mother. It was agreed that Michael would be supported by a keyworker in the residential unit who would, in turn, consult with one of the therapists from the adolescent psychiatric unit. It was also agreed that the IT worker would be a joint keyworker and help to devise social and recreational activities with Michael.

Third placement breakdown
In his second week at the local residential unit there was a violent incident in which a resident was punched and kicked by Michael and a new member of staff was threatened and pushed hard against a wall. Michael rushed out of the unit and returned home.

Fourth placement breakdown

The following week Michael dropped into the IT centre in the hope of finding his IT keyworker, got into a fight with another boy and threatened two of the centre staff. Michael was suspended from the centre for a month.

The IT keyworker was worried about Michael and tried to keep contact with him but short of wandering the streets looking for him there seemed to be little chance of this happening and he had a young offenders programme and a summer playscheme to run.

In this case the following processes can be observed:

1. The young person behaves in a way which is a flagrant invitation or challenge to members of the professional network to 'do something about it'.
2. The level of anxiety of members of the professional network rises.
3. More people are invited to join the professional network, usually in excess of the 'minimum sufficient' number necessary to do the job.
4. The expanded network opts for a solution which offers the highest level of containment to the young person and the greatest level of security to network members. The young person's needs take second place to the needs of the professional and managerial decision-makers who will be answerable for the decision if it goes wrong.
5. A decision which meets these professional and managerial imperatives is arrived at and the young person is placed in secure accommodation.
6. The level of anxiety of members of the professional network drops rapidly.
7. People now leave the professional network, usually in excess of the 'minimum sufficient' number necessary to do the job.
8. The situation breaks down and a lone worker is left, surrounded by the 'pieces', unsure whether, and if so how, she/he should/could pick them up again.
9. The situation drifts until the young person falls foul of the justice system or is picked up again by the psychiatric system.

From a situation in which he was inundated with professional 'help', Michael moves to another where he is effectively left to his own devices. This 'flood or drought' response to troublesome young people falls far short of the 'optimal' intervention advocated in this book.

An early warning system

It is clear from the example of Michael that the problem for practitioners and researchers is to identify those features of a social situation which indicate that things are 'getting out of hand' before they actually get out of hand. We need to identify them so that damage and disruption can be minimised and the processes can be understood and worked with.

One might choose to identify an administrative cut-off point when, for example, the young person is located in their third unplanned placement, as an indicator of a situation moving towards crisis. From our study, however, it appears that the best indicators that a situation is moving towards a crisis or 'flashpoint' are the heightened anxieties of the young person, and the members of the professional network who doubt that they will be able to control the young person's behaviour. In this situation, the adults and the young person lose contact with each other and communication between them is drastically reduced.

As we have seen, it is usually at this moment of peak anxiety that decisions to move a young person, or to place them in security are made. One of the major functions of this decision is to alleviate this anxiety. An alternative approach could be to introduce an individual or small team into the situation who would support the network and the young person in their attempts to devise a solution they can all 'live with'. They would, for a limited period of time, assume responsibility for the situation, thus freeing the young person and members of the network from the anxieties which 'freeze' them and stop them thinking creatively about the situation. They would undertake an analysis of the incident/s which had precipitated the crisis, highlighting those factors which had led the young person and the adults to their present predicament.

High anxiety situations are also high blame situations and it seems imperative that the relationship between the young person, the network and the individual/team which intervenes at the point of crisis should be a consultative rather than a managerial one.

At the second stage in this process there would be an attempt to hand the young person on to a 'natural' community network consisting, characteristically, of parents, teachers and local community figures; priests, mullahs, youth workers etc., while the professional network would remain in a sustaining role as an invisible-as-possible support system with flexible outreach potential.

A major limitation on the flexibility of official responses to young people in crisis is that most of the resources available to deal with the crisis are building-based. Thus, a young person in need of security must enter a secure unit and risk all the unintended consequences of such an admission. A spell in a secure unit is often seen by the young person and members of the professional network as an indication that the young person has reached the 'end of the road'. Yet, as we have already noted, time in a secure unit can also offer a refuge, time to think, time for a key worker to work intensively with a young person on issues of mutual concern.

In an attempt to avert the use of security and cut costs Essex County Council SSD introduced an experiment in which youngsters referred to security moved first to an open unit staffed at the level of a secure unit. Only if they proved uncontrollable in this setting were they moved on to security. There was a dramatic reduction in the use of security by social workers, the average length of time young people spent in security and, of course, the cost as well.

The other aspect of the building-based nature of services is that if these particularly vulnerable and volatile young people were to be attached to a worker or small team of workers, rather than a series of units or buildings, continuity, and hence their sense of security which is decimated by successive changes of placement, could be developed. This is the a model of work with difficult adolescents adopted by the Small Schools in Denmark. The key to the success of this endeavour, however, lies in the matching of the unit, the worker, the programme and the young person.

Matching

Research undertaken in Canada by Brill (1978) indicated that work with disturbed or 'dangerous' young people was most effective when the regime in which they were placed was geared to what he described as their 'conceptual level'. The idea of conceptual level does not describe intelligence, but rather, the capacity of an individual to cope with the complexities of their social environment.

He argued that in the progress of normal human growth and development people progress through a series of 'conceptual levels' and, as a result, are able to cope with social relationships of ever greater complexity. Brill identified four basic levels of development (see Table 6.1) but noted that people who are institutionalised or emotionally damaged often fail to progress beyond, or may regress to, a relatively low conceptual level.

Brill found that people who operated at levels B/C and B survived reasonably well if they were placed in a situation in which they were asked to cope with the type of environment designed for people operating at level A. People operating at level A who were placed in a situation characterised by the need to undertake the degree of abstract reflection and

The hard core

self-determination appropriate to people operating at level C, reacted in extreme and sometimes violent ways however. When matched to 'A environments' they coped very well. Beyond this however, the conceptual levels of A people placed in A environments tended to develop. Brill concluded that conceptual levels were not fixed but that inappropriate matching with a worker or an environment would prevent level A young people from developing socially.

Table 6.1   Conceptual level

Level	Some basic characteristics
A	Self-centred; unorganised; difficulty in planning; impulsive; limited control of emotions; easily confused; do not work out alternatives; cope with difficulties by denial; egocentric; reactive to authority.
B	Learning ground rules and social norms which apply to everyone; think in terms of good/bad, right/wrong; categoric thinking; rely on external standards; dependent on authority; concerned with rules; frequently opposed to change.
B/C	Learning about self and how one is *distinct* from others. Starts to generate own concepts; some conditional thinking; reliance on internal standards and emotions; takes into account two or more viewpoints simultaneously; deals with greater ambiguity; more assertive but not necessarily by aggression; interpersonal differentiation; can adapt to change.
C	Applying self-controls to an empathetic understanding of other persons and differences between them.

Of the eight young people in our study about whom we had sufficient information:

5 were operating at conceptual level A;
2 were operating at conceptual level B; and
1 was operating at conceptual level B/C.

All but one of these young people would, according to Brill, be unable to cope with settings which lacked clear rules and structures, required them to make complex choices or to deal with ambiguous relationships. Most of these young people had had a large number of placements and it is at least arguable that some of their placement breakdowns may have been occasioned by a mismatch with the setting in which they were placed or the style of work adopted by foster parents or key workers.

Brill's thesis helps to explain an apparent paradox we encountered in our study, which was that some of the young people who, on the face of it, were most thoroughly institutionalised and least able to discriminate and effect choices, fared very well when they left institutions.

Making it alone

It is a curious fact that the next move for troublesome adolescents who have exhausted the resources of the residential care system may be in one of two, dramatically different, directions. They may move into secure accommodation or out of the care system altogether into their own flat, bed and breakfast or a hotel; the total institution or complete freedom. Remarkably, the young people we studied who moved out of the care system appeared to fare remarkably well.

Successful independent living placements had the following characteristics:

1. There was frequent and flexible 'outreach' contact with a key worker from the Assessment Service or IT.
2. The young person was able to visit the original in-care placement on a 'drop-in' basis. They could, as it were, 'come home' to be 'looked after' on their own terms.
3. The keyworker focused on the identification of the young person's wants and needs with them and helped them to use their own, and other, available resources to get those wants and needs met.
4. The keyworker focused on finding solutions rather than elaborating problems.
5. The absence of the young person's peers, and peer group conflict and rivalry, meant that they were not under pressure to engage in the kind of acts of bravado that had got them into trouble in other placements.

These, and our other findings, have implications for policy and practice with young people held in, or at risk of entering, secure institutions. The form that such a policy might take is discussed in Chapter 8 of this book. Specific implications for policy and practice are given below.

The implications for policy and practice

1. A crisis consultancy team

The breakdown of a placement and a referral to secure accommodation marks a point of crisis in a highly charged social process which involves the young person and their professional and 'natural' networks. As such it would seem logical that an effective intervention at this point should mobilise what Skynner (1971) calls the 'minimum sufficient network'. He writes (p3):

> The word Network as I shall use it here, refers to a set of psychological structures which need to be connected to one another if the total system is to be autonomous — that is capable of intelligent response and adaptation .... The addition of the words Minimum Sufficient indicates that we must include as much of the network as is essential to achieve our aim ... .

In order to work in this way it is important that a worker, or team, from beyond the network/s should help to define, and then undertake work with members of the minimum sufficient network. It is therefore recommended that:

(a) A small consultancy team, of no more than six people in the first instance, be recruited from staff within the Adolescent Services Division. Their role is to enter and 'hold' situations which have developed into crises or to take hold of situations which are developing in this way. Like lifeboat persons they would pursue their usual careers but an allowance for their consultancy activities might be built into their workloads.

(b) Membership of this team would change by rotation thus allowing all divisional staff to gain experience of being part of it.

(c) The consultancy team would receive training in work with networks, large groups and systems.

(d) Other divisional staff would receive training in the use of consultancy.

(e) The clearest possible criteria for when and how the consultancy team was to be involved in situations should be devised in consultation with divisional staff.

(f) The team would work to a senior manager in the division who would mandate them to 'hold' crisis situations.

2. Assessment

At present assessment tends to be individualised and as a result fails to provide the type of information which could inform a 'systemic' intervention of the type outlined above. It is therefore recommended that a new format for assessment be devised which includes information about:

(a) the sequence of events which led to, and apparently precipitated, the crisis;

(b) recent events in the establishment or centre in which the young person is placed;

(c) the staff/resident ratio at the establishment or centre;
(d) the quality of staff/resident relationships at the establishment or centre;
(e) the quality of the relationships between the young person and the staff at the establishment or centre;
(f) The ethos/philosophy and methods adopted at the establishment or centre;
(g) significant events in the young person's professional network; conflict, loss, humiliation etc.;
(h) significant events in the young person's 'natural network'; conflict, loss, humiliation etc.;
(i) the characteristics, in terms of the 'conceptual level' demanded by the setting which is both best suited to a young person's present level of functioning and will enable them to develop a more sophisticated level of functioning;
(j) the style of work/worker best suited to a young person's present level of functioning and the style of work/worker which will enable them to develop a more sophisticated level of functioning.

3. Matching workers with young people
It would follow from this that:

(a) A small team of 'keyworkers' be recruited from within the Adolescent Services Division.
(b) These workers would be 'matched' with young people and free to work across settings utilising whatever methods are from time to time appropriate.
(c) They would be mandated and managed by the consultancy team who might also offer supervision and consultancy to the group.

4. Class, race and gender
It would appear that class, race and gender determine the system into which a young person is inserted, the ways in which their problems are defined and what happens to them within systems. Too often this means that the most deprived young people, because they are inserted into a low-status system, are further deprived because they lack access to other forms of help which might be appropriate to their needs. It is therefore recommended that:

(a) A consideration of the appropriateness of a placement/referral in terms of the class, race, and gender of the young person become a routine part of decision-making.
(b) Case reviews consider whether alternative and more appropriate responses to a young person's difficulties can

be found in other statutory, voluntary or private educational, recreational, therapeutic or helping facilities.
(c) The Division maintains an up-to-date and exhaustive directory of such facilities.
(d) The contribution of racism and sexism to friction, conflict and absconding in units and establishments be monitored and reported back to the consultancy group on a routine basis.

5. Diversion from security

The scheme pioneered in Essex in which young people referred to a secure unit enter a heavily-staffed non-secure unit in which attempts are made to salvage the broken-down situation they have left would appear to have much to commend it. Not least, it appears to offer support and containment without the stigma of being 'locked up'. It is therefore recommended that:

(a) When established, the consultancy team explore the viability of a diversion from the security unit as the base from which their interventions might be launched.

Conclusion

This chapter argues neither for the blanket interventionism envisaged by the protagonists of welfare in the 1960s nor for the 'radical non-intervention' of the late 1970s and 1980s. Instead, it proposes an 'optimal' intervention shaped by a young person's needs, predicament and stated wishes, and geared to his or her emotional and conceptual capacities. In placing the individual at the centre of the intervention, it nonetheless recognises the need to address the organisational inertia and institutionalised prejudice which may have a decisive impact on the destinies of young people caught up in the child care, justice, special educational and adolescent psychiatric systems. It also says that under the right circumstances, social work can help young people in crisis and that, we think, is worth remembering.

References

Becker 1963 *Outsiders: Studies in the Sociology of Deviance*. Free Press
Brill R 1978 Implications of the concept level matching model for treatment of delinquents. *Journal of Research in Crime and Delinquency*, **12** 229–246
Burney E 1985 *Sentencing Young People*. Gower
Cicourel A 1968 *The Social Organisation of Juvenile Justice*. Wiley
Curtis S 1989 *Juvenile Delinquency — Prevention through Intermediate Treatment*. Batsford

De La Motta C 1984 *Blacks in the Criminal Justice System*. Unpublished MA thesis Aston University

Denne J 1990 Transinstitutionalisation. *Youth Social Work* **2**, Winter 1990–91

Dennington J 1987 *The Use of Secure Accommodation*. Unpublished MSc thesis Brunel University

Farrington 1984 England and Wales. In Klein M (ed) *Western Systems of Juvenile Justice*. Sage

Gelsthorpe L 1983 Images of the Female Offender *Journal of the London IT Assn*. Autumn, 3–9

Goffman I 1968 *Asylums*. Penguin

Griffith R 1988 Community Care: An Agenda for Action. HMSO

Hoghugi M, Nethercott S 1977 Troubled and Troublesome. *Aycliffe Studies in Problem Children* 59–60

Holman R 1976 *Inequality in Child Care*. CPAG

Landau S 1981 Juveniles and the police *Brit J Crim* **21** 143–72

Lupton C, Roberts G 1982 *On Record — Young People appearing before a Juvenile Court*. SSRIU

Matthews R 1989 *Review of Juvenile Justice in Tower Hamlets*. Unpublished

Mead G H 1934 *Mind, Self and Society*. University of Chicago Press, Chicago

Millham S et al. 1975 *After Grace, Teeth*. Chaucer

Millham S 1978 *Locking up Children*. Saxon House

NACRO 1988 *Appeals Against Custodial Sentences in Juvenile Courts*. NACRO

NACRO 1989 *Final Report on the IT Initiative Monitoring Exercise*. NACRO

Parker H et al 1989 *Unmasking the Magistrates*. Open University Press

Personal Social Services Council 1979 *A Future for Intermediate Treatment*. PSSC

Pinder R 1984 *Probation Work in a Multi-Racial Society: A Research Report*. Applied Anthropology Group, Leeds University

Pitts J 1986 Black youth and crime some unanswered questions. In Matthews R, Young J, *Confronting Crime*. Sage

Pitts J 1988 *The Politics of Juvenile Crime*. Sage

Pitts J 1990 *Camden Juvenile Resource Team Consultative Document*. Unpublished

Pitts J, Robinson T 1983 *Young Offenders in Lambeth*. LITA

Rutherford A 1986 *Growing Out of Crime*. Penguin

Skynner R 1971 The minimum sufficient network. *Social Work Today* August

Smith D 1983 *Police and People in London*. Policy Studies Institute

Stevens P, Willis C 1979 *Race, Crime and Arrests*. Home Office

Taylor W 1982 Black youth white man's justice. *Youth in Society* November 14–17

Thorpe D et al. 1980 *Out of Care*. George Allen and Unwin

Tipler J 1985 *Juvenile Justice in Hackney*. Hackney Social Services Dept.

7 Running out of care: developing a service for runaways

David Crimmens

> This chapter describes the development of Central London Teenage Project, Britain's first safe house for young runaways. The practice at the Project is analysed as an alternative model of working with young people, within the context of concerns about failure within the present child care system. The potential for future practice within the 1989 Children Act is anticipated. The chapter concludes that real choice needs to be available for young people and their families if the optimistic expectations of the new legislation are to be realised.

The Children's Society opened the Central London Teenage Project (CLTP) the first safe house for young runaways in June 1985. This unique initiative aimed to accommodate young people under the age of 17, or if they were in care up to the age of 19, who had run away to London. It aimed to investigate the reasons why young people ran away and find acceptable care and accommodation for them in partnership with their carers. Beyond this it proposed to return young people to their home area, or an alternative placement, as quickly and effectively as possible. The Project was also concerned to collect data to establish the numbers of young people who run away and their reasons for doing so.

More than 1200 young runaways have stayed at CLTP in the five years since it opened. Each young person has a unique story but one which illustrates many of the problems faced by vulnerable young people growing up in contemporary society. What they share is that they have taken the potentially dangerous step of running away from their families or local authority care and they have ended up in the West End of London. Often alone, they lack the experience and resources to fend for themselves and they are consequently vulnerable to abuse and exploitation.

The problem of young runaways has a long history. The best known is probably Oliver Twist whose life in Victorian England is so eloquently chronicled by Charles Dickens. 'Johnny Go Home' a documentary made by Yorkshire Television thrust the plight of the young single homeless in London before the public gaze. The programme also indicated that there was a younger group of 'runaways', who had additional difficulties by virtue of their age. The Law assumes that young people are not able to live independently until the age of 16. They are legally required to be in full-time education, and are therefore unable to undertake work, and are ineligible for independent income support even if 'estrangement' can be proved. As a result they are unlikely to legitimately occupy council or private accommodation. Their legal status as dependents is reflected in the statute which requires the police to detain anyone under 17 if they believe them to be in physical or moral danger.

Thus, a runaway can be defined as (De'ath 1986):

> A young person aged under 17 years or in local authority care, who has left home or residential care of their own accord but without agreement or is forced to leave and is missing for one or more nights.

The key issues in defining a young person as a runaway are the absence of parental permission and the age-related protection embodied within legislation.

Prior to the establishment of CLTP agencies working with the young single homeless in the West End of London were concerned about their inability to offer a service to young runaways because the legal status of these young people prevented them from providing accommodation. The evidence they collected, however, indicated that there were significant numbers of young people who were not being helped. Many of these young people were being picked up by the police, deemed to be 'at risk' and returned to where they had run away from. Nothing was done to address the problems from which these young people had run. This often resulted in them re-appearing in the West End within a short space of time, having learnt to keep their heads down when the police were around. Concern about the absence of appropriate help led to discussions between the Metropolitan Police, the responsible local authority and the Children's Society, out of which came the idea of a 'Safe House'.

The involvement of the Children's Society in this process was crucial. Founded in 1871 by Edward Rudolf as 'The Church of England Incorporated Society for Providing Homes for Waifs and Strays', it had a long and close connection with the Churches of England and Wales. The Society had respectability and credibility as a well-established organisation with a history of work with marginalised children and young people. It is also a large organisation with a social work and fund-raising presence in much of England and Wales. This provided a source of potential

Running out of care 115

funding for the new initiative while the credibility of the Society guaranteed public support. This was particularly important because of the questionable legality of work with young runaways. The testing-out of the legal issues required an organisation with such respectability, status and public support.

The process of putting together a Project which was unique and of dubious legality was a lengthy one. Advisers from the Social Services Inspectorate, the Children's Regional Planning Committee and the Children's Legal Centre were involved in an Advisory Group which struggled with the legal issues of harbouring runaways and the recovery of children who had runaway from care. A major area of concern was the proposal to establish a confidential address which would not be available to parents, guardians or the social workers of young runaways. In the event the Children's Society adopted a high risk strategy and invested resources in this first safe house for young runaways.

CLTP accommodates up to ten young people, male and female, in a four-storey house in an ordinary London street. Most of them have their own bedroom though some prefer the security of sharing with a friend. There are no domestic staff at the Project and young people are expected to participate in cleaning and the preparation of meals. The Project is staffed 24 hours each day, 365 days a year and receives new referrals at any time of the day or night. The Project team consists of a Project Leader, three Senior Project Workers, seven Project Workers, and other workers who provide research and administrative back-up. The permanent staff is supported by locum workers. The team is multi-disciplinary including people experienced and professionally qualified in the field of social work, youth and community work, teaching and psychiatric nursing.

Gaining young people's trust is crucial. Young people stay at the Project because it offers them a breathing space and an alternative to survival on the street. The house is 'safe' because young people stay at the Project by choice. An overriding fear for many young runaways is that parents, social workers or the police will turn up on the doorstep and take them home against their will. This is the main reason that the address of the Project is confidential. The principle and practice of a confidential address has been a contentious one, and some social workers have objected to it. Telephone contact is encouraged however and facilities are available for meetings on 'neutral territory' between young people and their carers.

The Project strives to involve young people in making decisions about their future. Experience over the past five years indicates that the Project can be helpful in providing a bridge between young people and their carers. The Project acknowledges the difficulties which many young people have in communicating with adults and recognises that young people may have had difficult relationships with carers. 'Breathing space' and the skilful crisis intervention of Project staff provide time and assistance in helping young people to say what is troubling them and what they feel they will need in the future.

The referral process

The role of the Social Services Emergency Duty Team which serves the West End of London, is crucial in the referral process. Initially, the police referred young runaways they regarded as being at risk or who had gone into the police stations asking for help, direct to the Project. Since 1987 however the police have referred these young people to the social services department. This change resulted from difficulties experienced by the Metropolitan Police in making direct referrals in a situation of questionable legality. The Project has worked very closely with the social services department and has an agreement with it to provide for young runaways found in its area. For its part the social service department has seen its responsibility as going beyond simply returning young runaways to their homes. This stance has been fundamental to the development of the Project.

The number of young runaways who refer themselves to the Project has steadily increased over the period the Project has been open. A small number hear of the Project through their own networks, but an increasing number have previously stayed at CLTP. Some of these young people have left the Project without an appropriate resolution being achieved and have returned to the street. Others have returned to the parental home or care, and found that this was unsatisfactory. They return to the Project for further help. This is particularly true of victims of sexual abuse.

On arrival each young person is interviewed by a Project worker and is asked to complete a simple form. As soon as possible after admission, the Missing Person's Bureau of the Metropolitan Police is informed that the young person is at the Project. In this way it is possible to ascertain whether the young person has been notified as a 'missing person'. Police in the young person's area of origin are contacted and asked to notify carers that the young person is safe and to give them the Project telephone number to encourage contact.

The co-operation of the police has been fundamental to the survival and development of CLTP. They have participated in the Advisory Group, sorted out problems with police colleagues in other parts of the country, validated the Project and reinforced the importance of the confidential address.

Why do young people run away?

There is little specific research on young runaways in this country. In the USA, by contrast, researchers have attempted to develop typologies and explain the phenomenon. These explanations tend to focus on the characteristics of individual young people who run away, comparing these characteristics with those of a non-runaway adolescent population. Terms like 'crisis escapists' and 'unhappy runners' (Adams 1980) seem to be closest to the Project experience of young people who are running away from something. Adams contrasts these groups with 'casual hedonists' who run away from home to the bright lights. CLTP has very little experience of the latter group, though the Project does provide the occasional overnight stay with return rail fare the following morning. Social isolation, rejection and alienation are far more common characteristics of the young runaways admitted to CLTP. In his overview of American research Adams identifies the following as the most common characteristics of young runaways.

— Poor parent–child relations
— Extreme family conflict
— Alienation from parents
— Inter-personal tension
— Poor communication with parents
— School problems
— Physical abuse and neglect
— Incestuous relations with a family member
— Delinquency

It is useful to compare this with the characteristics of young people admitted to CLTP.

	1987	1988
Problems with parents	67	81
Unhappiness in care	49	47
Problems at school	8	12
Boredom	6	3
Abuse	8	4
Visiting London	8	13
Looking for work	12	7
Bullying	6	2
Court case	6	3
Pregnancy	0	1
Other	25	19
Don't know	6	18

It is interesting, though unsurprising, that such a high number would account for their running away in terms of 'problems with parents' and 'unhappy in care'.

Problems with parents

Child development theory and research continues to emphasise the importance of the family and relationships with parents during adolescence (Rutter 1975). Ideally the family provides a secure base from which the young person can safely explore their social world. While emphasis has recently been placed on the impact of marital breakdown and divorce on children and young people, it is disharmony and disruption which is likely to have most impact. Parental arguments and quarrels can produce a conflict of loyalties for the young person which they may find very difficult to cope with.

The following biographies are based on case material drawn from individual files at CLTP. They are not the experiences of any individual young person.

> Jenny was 14 years old when she ran away from a comfortable home in the South West. An only child, a successful pupil at the local grammar school, she packed her bags and ran away to London while both parents were at work. Arriving at Victoria Station she was approached by a man who offered to give her a bed and somewhere to stay. Fortunately this man was known to the Transport Police who arrested him and referred Jenny to the Safe House. Jenny told Project workers that she was fed-up with the arguments at home and sick of being picked on by both parents, who would not allow her to do the things that all her friends were allowed to do. Her list included smoking cigarettes and going to the local youth club. Jenny initially refused to talk to her parents, who were persuaded to give her a couple of days breathing space at the Project. They said they recognised that things had not been good for Jenny recently and that they were aware that this was due to problems they were having in their marriage. They said that they were going to arrange to see a counsellor. Being told this Jenny burst into tears and agreed to have a chat. She asked her parents if they would come and collect her. A meeting was held outside the local tube station in the parents' car and Jenny returned home. She had been missing for just over 36 hours.

85 per cent of young people who come to CLTP return to where they have run away from within a week.

Not all such stories have a happy ending. Parents are not always able to take their share of the responsibility. Some blame their children for the problems in the family and say that they do not want them back. In these circumstances negotiations have to take place with local authority social services departments about taking parental responsibility. One common problem occurs in reconstituted families where, usually, mother's new partner has difficulty in being accepted by adolescent sons or daughters. Mother may be faced with a choice between the partner and her child and this can produce extremely difficult situations for young people. Rivalry between boys and their mother's new partners can result in violence. Girls may experience difficulties including becoming the victims of sexual abuse.

Unhappy in care

In 1989/1990, 54 per cent of the young people referred to CLTP had run from home and 43 per cent had run from local authority care. Slightly more young women than young men ran from care. The recent period has seen a steady increase in the numbers of 14 and 15 year old sexually-abused young women in care referred to CLTP from the West End of London. These are the young people with the most severe difficulties and they are far more likely to spend protracted periods of time in the safe house than other runaways.

The list of problems which young runaways from local authority care bring with them is all too familiar and has been more than adequately documented by 'Who Cares', 'NAYPIC' and 'The Children's Legal Centre'. These relate to the discrepancies between the care system in principle and the care system in practice. Young people do not feel listened to, they do not feel that their opinions, ideas, thoughts and feelings are taken into account when plans are being made for their future. They do not feel that there is anybody they can turn to with these grievances. Young people in care are often not invited to important meetings and statutory case reviews, if these take place, but are expected to accept the decisions made at these meetings. In addition, many young people in care continue to experience difficulties with the unresolved problems within their own families, conflict with, or rejection by, natural parents and the absence of consistent adults, whether social workers or foster parents.

> Danny, aged 15 years, ran away from his foster parents in the Midlands. He had been in care for the previous two years and during that time had stayed in the local assessment centre, two children's homes and with four sets of foster parents. Danny acknowledged that he had not been able to settle and he wanted to go back and live with his mother. Danny had been taken into care because his mother said she could not control him. Problems had started when mother's boyfriend moved in when Danny was eleven. Mother now had two new children and felt she could not cope with Danny 'at the moment'. A meeting was arranged which involved Danny's social worker, foster parents, mother and mother's boyfriend. Mother told Danny that she did not think that he could ever come home. The family was settled now and mother said that Danny was too much trouble. Danny is now 16 years old and will move into his own flat on his 17th birthday. Since the meeting he has ran back to CLTP on

a number of occasions to sort out various things that have been troubling him but he now feels more settled in a 'preparation for independence' unit.

One major problem presented by young runaways from care is the breakdown of foster placements. These young people often state quite clearly that they do not want to live in a family. They have families of their own which they may or may not return to. They do not want the pressures of family life, other adults 'pretending to be their mum or dad', or simply to continue to live in a situation in which they feel they have failed. What they want is a 'good children's home'.

This issue is discussed further below and in Chapter 4 of this book. It is important to note that in as much as we recognise that there is no such thing as a national juvenile justice system, just local systems, there is also no such thing as a national child care system (Thorpe et al. 1980, Ross and Bilson 1989). Although legal statute provides the framework within which systems develop, the quality of provision and practice in child care is piecemeal. What a young person actually receives is often dependent on where they live.

The proportion of children and young people in the population who are in local authority care is at an all-time low. It is argued that young people in care at present are the most difficult, and have the most intractable problems. While there is an element of truth in this it is also the case that a smaller in-care population should enable us to provide a higher quality of service. In reality some residential provision is little better than that offered by Victorian workhouses.

Project practice principles: listening

CLTP tries to help young people to help themselves. All Project practice aims to empower young people. Young people need to learn to start solving their own problems. Project workers engage with young people in this process rather than working on their behalf. Active listening is a fundamental principle of social work practice and as such is emphasised in all training courses. Yet because social workers with statutory responsibility may know that there are very few choices available to young people, they may have very little incentive to listen.

We work on the assumption that the young person's own views are of crucial importance, so giving young people time to talk is fundamental to our work. We listen to what the young person has to say and the way they want to say it. It is interesting to note that recently the NSPCC has compaigned under the banner 'Listening to Children' suggesting that this is the cornerstone of effective work with victims of sexual abuse. They advocate listening, hearing and validating' the point of view of children and young people (Blagg et al. 1989).

There is a need to acknowledge that the tendency to impose an adult perspective on a young person may effectively invalidate and consequently disempower them. Project practice focuses on enabling young people to take some responsibility for determining what should happen to them in the future.

Critics of this position argue that listening is insufficient. Young people must have feedback which tells them what to do, which points out the reality of a world which is essentially constructed by adults. Yet listening, hearing and validating is not an uncritical process. Project workers recognise that young people may not always know what they want. They may be confused. They may be experiencing a degree of disturbance, distress or chaos which makes it difficult for them to present a clear, cohesive and rational point of view. Young people may also propose solutions which are unrealistic or illegal, like having a flat at 14 years of age without adult supervision. The Project worker's task is to listen and hear what is being proposed, to reflect upon the advantages and disadvantages of a course of action and to work alongside a young person who is struggling to find a solution which is acceptable. It is our experience that imposed or forced solutions do not work. They do not last and without the commitment of the young person they are likely to lead to further episodes of running away.

It is important to acknowledge the relative privilege that workers have at CLTP which can be used to create a more equal relationship with young people. The Project as a 'refuge' stands to one side of the problematic reality from which a young person has run and reduces the pressure on them to be or do something. This helps the young person to explore what might be possible with Project workers as adults with whom they have an essentially short-term, non-statutory informal relationship. While there is still a power relationship between the adult worker and the young person it is different from that between the young person and their parents or social worker. The nature of this relationship determines what gets said by young people.

Project workers have nothing to sell apart from a commitment to engage young people in sorting out their futures. The local authority social worker as a 'broker' of resources may, by contrast, be selling products which many young people do not want to buy.

Advocacy

The question of what constitutes advocacy in a child care situation is contentious. The term embodies the concepts of negotiation, mediation and reconciliation, and as such presumes that the interests of young people may not always be the same as those of their parents or social workers.

Advocacy is rooted in questions of the rights of children and young people. Legislation emphasises adult obligations to work in the 'best interests' of young people, yet the young person's perspective can be directly at odds with the adult's assumptions about what constitutes such 'best interest'. Young runaways are underage and there are things which they cannot legally do yet Project workers must struggle to find ways of articulating the dilemmas and putting forward a young person's point of view.

The situation is further compounded by the existence of conflicting ideologies which emphasise on the one hand the salvation or protection of the child or young person and on the other the right of the child or young person to self-determination. This is a debate about the allocation of power and responsibility between the State and the family. Mnookin and Szwed (1983) emphasise age as the crucial factor in this debate. They maintain that to assert that age, unlike gender and race, is irrelevant to legal autonomy is to ignore biological and economic reality. Thus a child or young person can only have a level of autonomy which is related to their age and they therefore exist in a situation of structured dependency. As Freeman (1987) acknowledges:

> The very limited capacity of small children and the rather fuller if incomplete capacities of older children and adolescents.

Advocacy involves deciding who is to represent the child and how they are to do it in a situation of tension between what the young person wants and what the parents and social workers want. Experience at CLTP indicates that the principal concern of many parents is that their child is safe. Project workers then work with the implicit or explicit permission of parents to negotiate reconciliation. In cases where there is a high level of conflict between a young person and their parents, it is unlikely that progress towards reconciling them with their parents and returning them home will be made without the help of a social worker.

Working relationships between CLTP and social workers with care responsibilities for young people can be complex. It appears that social workers as the 'responsible' or 'administrative' parent with prescriptive responsibilities do not want to make mistakes for which they may be held accountable. Research into social workers' opinions of the Safe House (Crimmens 1989) indicates a largely positive view of safe housing for young runaways. However, this research indicated a range of concerns which illustrate many of difficulties which afflict attempts to offer effective advocacy for young people in local authority care.

Section 18 of the Child Care Act 1980 requires that:

> In reaching any decision relating to a child in their care a local authority shall give first consideration to the need to safeguard and to promote the welfare of the child throughout his childhood and shall so far as practicable ascertain the wishes and feelings of the child regarding the decision and give due consideration to them, having regard to his age and understanding.

Freeman (1983) maintains that children in care are given too little independence and too little responsibility.

> Childhood should be an apprenticeship when the skills of living are acquired; for children in care this is all too rarely the case.

He acknowledges that there are grounds for qualified optimism, but notes that there is often a greater discrepancy between what ought to happen, even in terms of what is prescribed in Statute and Government Circulars, and what actually happens in practice. The absence of mandatory checks mean that many young people, unable to redress their grievances in care, may end up running away.

If we compare the following statement (BASW 1977):

> The child in care has a right for information concerning his circumstances and to participate in the planning of his future.

With the assertion that (Page and Clark 1977):

> All we need to get over is we ought to be able to have a say in who is there discussing our lives. We ought to be able to speak for ourselves. And if we can't get our points across ... we ought to have a spokesman for ourselves. Why don't the children have their own person they want to speak for them?

We see the gap between what ought to be and what is very clearly.

It is important to recognise the limitations of the Statutory Review which is often more of an administrative procedure than a genuine dialogue. It would appear that there is a potential conflict of role for many social workers between effectively carrying out the agreed procedures of the local authority and their 'professional' task as a social worker. This conflict may be compounded by personal and professional antipathy towards work with adolescents, the relatively low status of such work and the high levels of responsibility it sometimes imposes.

Beyond this, many social workers have great difficulty with the idea of the confidential address of the safe house and feel disempowered by the apparent lack of trust implied in the practice of refusing to disclose the whereabouts of the young runaway.

When a social worker who carries statutory responsibility for a young person is stripped of the capacity to discharge that responsibility he or she may well come to see the Project as an unnecessary, unwelcome and unjustified interference. Relationships between the Project and social services departments can become polarised. As a result, the attempt to act as advocates for young people has sometimes involved the Children's Society in extensive and expensive litigation in the High Court.

Research

CLTP has been fortunate in having a full-time research worker attached to the team. The history of the first two years of the Project is documented in *Young Runaways: Findings From Britain's First Safe House* (Newman 1989). The book describes in some detail the process of setting up the Project and how it has been run. Its great strength lies in the case histories which enable young runaways to account for their experience in their own words. This attempt to allow the client to speak provides an authentic basis for practice development (Mayer and Timms 1970). It also offers powerful evidence which has been used in attempts to influence social policy. Current research focuses on the system careers of young runaways and systems failure in the areas from which they have run.

Organisational strategies: addressing injustice

The corporate strategy of the Children's Society emphasises the importance of doing more than providing services. The Society is committed to gathering together experiences from practice in order to challenge structures, systems and policies which disempower and disadvantage children and young people.

CLTP is a good example of this strategy. Significant effort has been devoted to bringing the issue of runaways to the attention of policy makers and the public. This strategy utilises the traditional networks of the organisation and a growing Public Relations Department to raise the profile of this issue. The Children's Society has made a major commitment to advocating for amendments to Child Care Law with respect to young people who run away. Research findings from CLTP, the only Project in the country working with young runaways, have been used consistently to raise public concern about the issue. The Social Policy Unit spent many hours talking to MPs about the organisation's experience of work with young runaways. Over 12 000 supporters of the Children's Society wrote to their MPs during the passage of the Children Bill through Parliament, expressing their concern about the plight of young runaways and asking that provision be made within the new legislation to help these young people. This strategy has been successful in generating concern for the plight of young runaways and the 1989 Children Act provides a clear legal framework for *Refuges for children at risk* (DoH 1990).

Marginality

Young people by virtue of their age and lack of economic autonomy live in a world of structural dependency. This world consists of relationships within the family, kinship and neighbourhood networks, peer group and with other significant adults like school teachers and youth workers. Running away removes the young person from the relative safety of this world. Although the runaway may be escaping from psychological, emotional and physical dangers within these networks, they are also leaving behind important sources of psychological, emotional and physical support.

Many young people, particularly girls, run away in pairs and retain the important support of an existing friendship. Others are fortunate enough to be 'looked after' by some of the peer networks which exist on the street. The act of running away marginalises all runaways. The experience can compound the very difficulties they have run away from. The Project records contain many horror stories. These illustrate the actual and potential dangers involved in running away. Being out on the street without a place to sleep, tired, hungry and cold, marginalises the young runaway. They have no legitimate access to resources in their own right. They suffer the same degree of physical marginality as their contemporaries who are young and homeless, but they are in an even worse situation being ineligible for any form of income support or housing. They become easy prey for those who would abuse and exploit them. The promise of a warm bed and a hot meal may lead a young runaway to engage in activities like prostitution, drink and drug abuse and begging which can have a fundamental impact on their self-image and self-esteem Chapman and Cook (1988) maintain:

> Individuals with a marginalised status will have to contend with perceptions and behaviour towards them which are likely to induce negative effects on their feeling of self-worth or self-esteem. Their personal perceptions of status inferiority, hopelessness and despair, are likely to contribute to the perpetuation of feelings of exclusion.

Sandy aged 15 ran away from home in an Outer London Borough. The only child of professional parents, she was having difficulty at school where she was regarded as a 'rebel'. She met a group of young people who were hanging around Piccadilly. They told Sandy about Centrepoint where some of them were staying. However, somebody told her that Centrepoint would send her back to her parents because she was underage. Late in the evening Sandy became separated from this group. It was raining and Sandy was cold. She had spent her last couple of pounds on a hamburger and chips. A young man approached her and suggested they go for a drink. Sandy agreed. The young man was friendly and sympathetic. He said he had had difficulties himself with his parents when he was younger. The young man told Sandy he shared a flat with his sister and that he was sure that his sister wouldn't mind Sandy staying for a couple of days until things were sorted out with her parents. Sandy went back to his flat. His sister was not at home. Sandy was already a little intoxicated and agreed to try the drugs which were offered. She was given a cocktail of 'Speed' and 'Acid' and violently raped by the young man. In the morning his friend arrived. He raped Sandy. She was kept a prisoner all day while the two young men continued to abuse her. They fell asleep later in the evening intoxicated with drink and drugs. Sandy escaped. In the early hours of the following morning she arrived at CLTP.

The very experience of running away and life on the street can increase the young person's marginality. This can result in feelings of emotional and psychological distance on top of the initial reality of physical distance. Young people may come to feel that they are unable to return to mainstream society even if that is what they really want to do.

The future

The 1989 Children Act provides a legal framework for organisations like the Children's Society to work with young runaways. It also provides official recognition that there is a problem. The legislation provides the potential for partnership in the development of services which are user-friendly to actual and potential runaways, which could reduce the likelihood of young people running away.

The Children's Society is developing a number of projects. A Safe House has been open in Bournemouth for the past two years and a new Safe House is scheduled to open in Leeds in early 1991. Projects in Birmingham, Manchester and Newport in Gwent are working with young people on the street. Experiments using 'safe families' to help young runaways are developing. Five years after CLTP first opened, more is known about the number of missing dogs than the numbers of missing children and young people in Britain. Research carried out in England and Wales by the Children's Society indicated that more than 98,000 young people run away each year. The Society believes that this may

Running out of care

well be an under-estimate. Practice at CLTP indicates that many of the young people who arrive at the Project have not been notified as missing to the police.

The 1989 Children Act provides the legislative context for work with children and young people in the future. The idea of partnership with families will change the basis on which social work is practised. There will be new checks and balances which will provide a framework of rights. More decisions about the lives of young people will be made in the Courts where they, and their parents, will have a right to be legally represented. There is significant potential within the new 'procedure for representation' for empowering young people and their parents. Each local authority is required to establish procedures which must receive appropriate publicity. 'Representations' can be made by any child who is being looked after by that local authority, by any other child who is in need and by any other person who has sufficient interest in the child's welfare. This may include a parent, foster parent or any other person with parental responsibility. The representation procedure must have an independent element. Local authorities will be required to monitor their procedures to ensure that they comply with the representations regulations (DoH 1989).

This system could provide the kind of service developed by CLTP for many more young people. It should help to enhance the possibility of meaningful partnership. The proposed structure should increase the potential for young people and their families to put forward their point of view and have this acted on. The requirement for an independent element in the procedure provides a framework for more agencies like CLTP to engage in youth advocacy to more effectively represent the position of the young person.

The new legislation provides grounds for a renewed but cautions sense of optimism for the 1990s. There have been important and welcome developments during the 1980s which have questioned intervention by the state in the family. But we are aware that policies which emphasise non-intervention can easily become a legitimation for doing nothing.

The problems faced by marginalised young people like runaways continues to grow. Policy over the past decade appears to have focused on social control rather than welfare:

> It is all too easy for young people to escape into limbo: homeless, penniless and jobless, the responsibility of no agency and only the centre of any kind of attention when their behaviour becomes anti-social or criminal.

The responsibility to safeguard and promote the welfare of children in need is at the heart of the 1989 Children Act. It places welfare firmly back on the agenda and challenges us to look again at fundamental assumptions. The Act provides a broad framework and it will be up to each local child care system to determine what their priorities will be. Partnership with children, young people and their families may also require major shifts in professional attitudes and cultures.

We believe that CLTP has demonstrated the potential of a residential response to the problems faced by some young people. There are some indications that change is on the horizon. The National Children's Bureau research into Warwickshire's policy that 'Every child has a right to a family life' indicates that some thought is being given to the exclusivity of families as the primary placement strategy. There has been much adverse publicity and scandal about the state of residential care for young people. In the current climate it will be relatively easy to further reduce the availability of children's homes. The dramatic closure of all residential homes in Warwickshire appears to have been a useful experiment in that County, strategically well thought out and well resourced. This is not the case with some other authorities who have crudely attempted to operate a similar strategy.

Warwickshire now acknowledges that there is a need for some residential care. It is important that there is a change in perception of the value of residential care by both local authorities and field social workers. This is required to redress the situation in which research evidence in the late 1970s (DHSS 1985) indicated that it was the attitude of social workers as much as the fiscal crisis which led to the decline of residential care as a positive option for young people.

The challenge to social services departments working in conjunction with partners in the voluntary sector is to create a selection of services which pay due regard to young people's and parents' wishes. To deny choice is to deny justice to these young people and their families. Choice is a key issue and without choice many of the opportunities offered by the new legislation will not be realised. Those who have most need will receive poor and inappropriate services. It is essential that the residential option is available for young people who want it and that this is seen as a positive choice:

> No-one is saying that residential care is perfect, far from it. But it does have an important role to play, if we listen to what some of the young people who have been through the system are telling us.

References

Adams G 1980 Runaway youth projects: comments on care programs for runaways and throwaways. *Journal of Adolescence* 3

Blagg H, Hughes J, Wattan C (eds) 1989 *Child Sexual Abuse: Listening Hearing and Validating the Experiences of Children*. Longman
British Association of Social Workers 1977 Charter of Rights for Children in Care. *Social Work Today* **8** (25)
Chapman T, Cook J 1988 Marginality, Youth and Government Policy in the 1980s. *Critical Social Policy* **8** (1)
Crimmens D 1989 *Reluctant Consumers: Social Worker Opinion on a Unique Service for Young Runaways*. Unpublished MSc Dissertation
De'ath E 1986 *Young People under Pressure: Runaways and Others*. Briefing Paper No: 1 The Children's Society
Department of Health 1989 *An Introduction to The Children Act*. HMSO
Department of Health 1990 *Refuges for Children at Risk. Guidance and Regulations*. Consultation Paper No. 6
Department of Health and Social Security 1985 *Social Work Decisions in Child Care. Recent Research Findings and their Implications*. HMSO
Freeman M 1983 The concept of children's rights. In Geach H, Szwed E. *Providing Civil Justice for Children*. Arnold
Freeman M 1987 Child care and the Law. In Stone W, Warren C *Protection or Prevention: A Critical Look at the Voluntary Child Care Sector*. National Council of Voluntary Child Care Organisations
Mayer J, Timms N 1970 *The Client Speaks*. Routledge and Kegan Paul
Mnookin R, Szwed E 1983 The best interests syndrome and the allocation of power in child care. In Geach H, Szwed E op cit
Newman C 1989 *Young Runaways: Findings From Britain's First Safe House*. The Children's Society
Page R, Clark G 1977 *Who Cares?* National Children's Bureau
Ross S, Bilson A 1989 *Social Work Management and Practice*. JKP
Rutter M 1975 *Helping Troubled Children*. Penguin Books
Thorpe D, Smith D, Green C, Paley J 1980 *Out of Care*. Allen and Unwin

8 Towards a policy for effective work with marginalised young people

Tim Bateman, John Dennington, Kath Kelly, Terry Lyons, Geoff Pick, John Pitts and Chris Stanley

> This chapter considers the relationship between policy management and practice. It identifies the distinctive characteristics of youth social work and specifies the ways in which thoughtful policies and sensitive management can facilitate effective practice.

In adolescence a person is usually moving away from school and out of the family. Having few or no dependents young people have less need to commit themselves fully to a job or a career. So, for a time they exist on the margins of these institutions, experiencing a relative freedom from constraint which can be both enjoyable and confusing. At its best, adolescence offers a moratorium, a period during which we can stand back from the people and institutions which have been so important in our lives and look at them critically.

If it works adolescence, and the marginality that comes with it, offers us the opportunity to work out the kind of adult we want to be. Adolescence is no more intrinsically problematic than childhood or middle age, each are periods of change and adjustment which can be got through very creatively if those around us are supportive and circumspect in the right proportions at the right times. This said, it has to be acknowledged that some adults find young peoples' tendency to question authority and disagree with the 'taken for granted', difficult, threatening and challenging. This does not always displease young people of course, since such behaviour tends to vindicate what they were saying about adults in the first place. The name of this game is 'renegotiating the boundaries' and it is how young people get the room they need to grow.

Working with 'normal' adolescents can, as a result, be a very emotive experience for adults who sometimes feel ambivalent about a young person's relative freedom from responsibility and their assertiveness. Working with young people who are 'at risk', in trouble, or in danger can be even more stressful because the renegotiation of boundaries can be far more frantic and the affront to authority far more challenging.

Youth social work is, on the one hand, about cutting through the testing and resistance in a non-threatening way in order to establish *contact*. On the other, it involves using that contact to offer the young person an appropriate degree of *containment* if they find themselves running out of control.

Protecting a young person from themselves or others, or defending others, including ourselves, against them is very stressful. In attempting to protect young people, we often work in a situation where we cannot remove them to a 'place of safety' and so have to live with the anxiety that their, or our own, vulnerability provokes. In our attempts to defend others we sometimes feel pressed to exert some control over young people in a situation in which the only obvious sanction available to us is the ultimate one of the removal of their liberty. It is not hard to see why youth social work is not a popular option.

It is clear that if we enter a situation with a protective or defensive brief, the role we play, and our anxieties about it, can militate against us making contact with the young person. Recently, a residential work staffing agency summoned one of its workers to a South London Adolescent Unit which had been experiencing difficulties. He was told that they needed 'a couple of hefty lads down there'. Not surprisingly, the excited and belligerent residents were waiting for him on the stairs when he arrived.

If we do not make contact, then the chances of offering some degree of containment, this side of a secure unit, are limited. Placing the young person in a secure unit under these circumstances may do no more than postpone the problem for a few days, after which they will be back on the street even less willing to engage with us.

We have highlighted *contact* and *containment* as two key aspects of the youth social work task and suggested that effective containment is dependent upon effective contact. Effective contact usually requires us to work on the client's issues at the client's pace, which means giving them room for manoeuvre or space. There are, however, a number of personal and organisational difficulties which must be confronted before such space can be created.

Some common problems in work with marginalised young people

The statutory relationship

An initial barrier to contact is the fact that the majority of the young people who come to the door of social services departments do so because they are subject to a statutory order of some sort. As a result they may well resent a social worker's involvement in their lives, seeing it as an unwarranted intrusion. A further consequence may be that some young people will test the boundaries of this relationship very vigorously by presenting threatening and self-damaging behaviour to the worker. This often makes workers frightened, yet as professionals they feel that they should be able to cope. As a result, they may develop a variety of, not always very useful, strategies to cope with the onslaught of the young person and the fear and anxiety it induces.

1. Splitting: deserving and undeserving adolescents

The psychological process of splitting people into those who are good and those who are bad is made easier by events which occur in the real world. At a simple level there is a tendency in most of us to feel a greater affinity with those who have been victimised rather than those who have perpetrated such victimisation. In work with difficult young people however this distinction becomes blurred as in the case of the sexually abused boy who proceeds to act out his own victimisation by abusing younger children. As a result our moral universe becomes confused.

Some of the young people referred to social workers can be readily integrated into alternatives to care and custody or other non-statutory youth provision and to that extent they can be brought in from the social margins. They may well have been involved in persistent, but not necessarily very serious, offending or truancy. Others, however, will have been involved in more serious, and possibly violent, behaviour. The responsiveness, or at least the willingness to co-operate, of the former group may then stand in sharp contrast with the resistance and often outright hostility of the latter. Whereas a viable social work plan can be constructed with the former group, it is often hard for the worker to imagine how they might begin to work with this latter group of marginalised young people. They defeat our ingenuity and can leave us feeling scared, confused and angry. No matter that they are themselves the victims of poverty, discrimination and abuse, it is as perpetrators that they present themselves to us.

A distinctive characteristic of the latter group is that they will have done this to most of the professionals they have previously met who, as a result, will have been unwilling to work with them. Although they will have been referred to a host of agencies and a multiplicity of placements it is quite likely that nobody will have made any significant contact with them. They will, as a result, bring to their encounter with the social worker a legacy of 'failed' placements and relationships and an expectation that this one will go the same way. If this fatalism is mirrored by that of the worker, it probably will.

Our problems are compounded by the fact that whereas the former group can usually be referred on to other agencies and other workers, the 'prognosis' of the latter group is so poor that, once allocated to us, we may fear that we will be 'stuck with them' until such time as the young person is taken out of circulation by the police or the courts. Indeed, as Parker et al. (1989) have noted, social workers may sometimes aid and abet this process by writing what they call 'vengeance reports'. It is hard for us as social workers to accept that sometimes our fear and anger about a client can result in such a vindictive response yet, in a situation in which human beings are unsupported and overstretched, it is hardly a surprising outcome.

Thus, workers may come to split the world into two; to bury the individuality of the young people with whom they work and to divide them instead into the deserving, who will co-operate with the social worker and make use of the services of the local authority, and the undeserving who reject them. Thus a hierarchy of marginality is created in which the 'undeserving' are further marginalised from the agents and agencies which might meet their needs.

2. Conservatism

There is an understandable tendency for those who carry statutory responsibility for difficult and dangerous young people to adopt fairly conservative forms of practice. The work can induce high anxiety and a siege mentality because decision-making in this area has an unavoidable element of risk associated with it. These risks include the risk to the worker's career in a situation where they will have to answer for what the volatile young people on their caseload may do to themselves or others.

Paradoxically such conservatism can lead to two quite different types of action, each of which will have undesirable consequences. At one extreme, the fear of making a wrong decision can result in the worker making no decision. The young person is effectively abandoned and left to their own devices. Youngsters may suddenly be catapulted into 'independent living' in a bedsit. Young people who have absconded from a placement may remain 'missing' for a long time even though workers know where they are, because the worker cannot be held responsible for what they do if she or he does not know where they are 'officially'.

At the other end of the spectrum lies recourse to physical confinement in secure accommodation or the abandonment of young people to custody as a result of the worker's failure to pursue the option of placement in an alternative-to-custody project.

In high anxiety situations decisions tend to be precipitated by crises and are, as a result, often made hastily. In the absence of a crisis decisions are delayed for fear of the consequences of a mistake. In both cases, decisions tend to be made without reference to the young person's needs and wishes.

As John Dennington (in Chapter 5 of this book) noted, there often seems to be little relationship between the behaviour or the social circumstances of the young people and whether they are placed in secure accommodation or bed and breakfast. Indeed, some young people will experience both approaches in quick succession, moving from bed and breakfast to a secure unit without, as it were, passing 'go'. The rationale for such placements must be sought in the anxieties of the workers and the availability of resources, not the behaviour of the young people.

As David Crimmens and the authors of Chapter 6 of this book observe, we need an optimum level of intervention which enables workers to negotiate a path between crisis responses and conservative non-intervention.

3. Conflict

A further feature of work with marginalised young people is the degree of conflict it tends to generate between professional workers within an agency and between agencies. This is not the place to explore the extent to which conflictual professional relationships are simply mirroring the conflictual nexus of relationships in which they are required to intervene. What is clear is that such conflict militates against the best interests of the young person.

In high stress situations, differences of opinion between workers about the most appropriate form of action can come to assume a far greater significance than they would, on the face of it, seem to merit. What might, in other circumstances, be seen as helpful advice can, in this situation, be received as unwarranted criticism and interference. The ever-present tendency for those with case responsibility to minimise risks can result in them resenting the 'interference' of 'outsiders' who have 'nothing to lose'. Even where responsibility is shared, anxiety can heighten disagreements about the value and likely outcomes of the strategies proposed. One of the consequences of this can be that in a situation which may require unity some workers will be more committed to the strategy than others. This can bring about a situation in which, for example, the field worker may be dutifully accompanying the young person and his parents to the family therapy sessions but the strategy is undermined because IT changes the time of the hobbies workshop the young person is supposed to attend and fails to tell them or the field worker.

These problems are compounded because there is no mechanism for resolving disputes or mediating, or negotiating a compromise, between professional peers. What happens is that when discussions reach, a usually very acrimonius, stalemate, either the idea of a shared strategy is abandoned or the problem is pushed up the hierarchy for, an inevitably unsatisfactory, management decision. If this latter option is pursued it then becomes possible to blame 'management' for yet another 'bloody stupid decision' and this can then reunite the professionals in their opposition to 'management'.

4. Reframing the problem by framing the problem-solvers

A further strategy for dealing with anxiety is reframing the problem. In this way the problem becomes, not the anxieties the young person evokes in us, but other workers who 'collude' with their 'bad behaviour' and 'undermine' our best efforts even though, on the face of it, they appear to be able to make contact with young people.

As such, these workers are in danger of being written off as 'over-involved', 'immature', 'collusive', 'mavericks', 'charismatic nuts' or 'cowboys' with 'authority problems'. More often than not, these people do not carry statutory responsibilities and have more time and more freedom to develop relationships. At a rational level this should make them an important resource for us in our attempts to work effectively with difficult young people. In fact, sometimes, we resent their privileged position and their apparent capacity to do with ease what we find so hard. Even though we may know that what they are able to do with young people is determined in large part by the roles they are able, or are not required, to play with them, this may not diminish the resentment we feel towards them.

These stereotypes are not simply based on fantasy, however. If we are not careful, work with marginalised adolescents can turn us inside out and split us down the middle. It can cause us to act like caricatures of ourselves. Whereas on the one hand we may be drawn into collusion with a young person who acts out the battle with authority which we never dared enter at the age of 16, on the other, we may be shocked to find ourselves responding exactly like our own parents did and we vowed we never would. In this context, maturity consists in recognising the immature or stultified parts of ourselves which are evoked by our encounter with a young person, accepting them and deciding how they will be kept under control. Maturity also involves standing back, separating the self from the problems and not getting riled by the inevitable testing-out. As Pitts (1990 p104) observes.

> It is hard to overstate the importance for the professional worker of not taking hurtful personal remarks personally. They are seldom, in the first instance at least, directed at us because of who we are but rather because of what we are. Wind-ups are seldom malicious, they are designed as a test to see how far we will go, how much we will take, and importantly, whether or not we have a sense of humour.

We must also confront the fact that we cannot work with everybody. This may be less important with some other client groups but in work with difficult young people such a recognition is vital. As the authors of Chapter 6 indicate, the evidence shows that the most effective work is done when the worker, the young person and the programme to be pursued are matched, where some element of worker choice is present and where good support and consultancy services are available.

Beyond this, is the reality that just as some people really do not want to, and should not be made to, work with under-fives so some people really do not want to work with adolescents. This is fine until they, or somebody else, feels that they *ought to*. But, as we know, *what is*, rather than *what ought to be*, is the only effective starting point for face to face work with marginalised young people.

Towards a policy for effective work with marginalised young people

Thus far, this chapter has dwelt upon the problems which workers in an SSD experience in their attempts to establish contact and work effectively with marginalised young people. It is the contention of this chapter that such work can be facilitated by a new kind of policy.

Such a policy would be both reactive and proactive, negative and positive. While, for example, it would act to promote radical 'non-intervention', in the cases of the young people identified in Chapter 6 who were unnecessarily imprisoned, it would also oppose the neglectful 'conservative non-intervention' which involved 'dumping' a youngster in bed and breakfast. Such a policy should moreover address the apparent paradox of workers demanding, on the one hand, the room and the autonomy to undertake creative and innovative practice while, on the other, they ask 'management' to give them more and more guidelines. This contradiction is however more apparent than real.

Good practice involves having space to work creatively and take calculated risks with young people who are difficult to engage, in the knowledge that managerial and professional support is available and that at certain junctures certain infallible procedures or gates will be invoked. These gates would, characteristically, concern receptions into, or discharges from, care, the initiation of care proceedings, placement, access to secure accommodation, SIR recommendations and decisions to withdraw a service or prosecute a young person in the wake of an assault upon staff.

Face to face practice, by contrast, cannot be rule-bound in this way. As a worker at the open forum complained, 'I sometimes think the authority is trying to script my interviews'. There may be some controversy about whether face-to-face work is an art, a science or a skill, but whatever it is, it certainly is not a bureaucratic procedure. Policy should reflect this by offering professional resources, and the time and space for face-to-face workers to demonstrate such skill, artistry and intellectual rigour. It should also support them in taking calculated risks if these are deemed to be in a young person's best interest.

It is confusion about the interplay between the areas of professional freedom and administrative constraint, the gates and the absence of support which provokes calls for ever more guidelines and the appointment of yet another 'specialist'. The other reason for such demands is that many workers feel alone and vulnerable in their work with marginalised young people. That they should sometimes feel like this because of the behaviour of the young people will be inevitable. That they should feel like this because of their fear of being blamed by their managers, or a public enquiry, if things go wrong is something which promotes conservative practice, and which an effective policy must address.

Corporatism

A distinguishing feature of this policy would be its commitment to corporate decision-making. Cases would be 'owned' by a group of workers and managers. On the basis of an agreed contract a worker would be mandated to undertake the face-to-face work with the young person. The mandate would specify the 'space' available to the worker and the contract would specify the resources at their disposal. This might include a commitment of supervision and consultancy sessions, the availability of an emergency bed or use of a minibus. The mandating group would act in a similar way to the workers behind the one-way screen in family therapy. At any one time a worker could be in the mandating group 'behind the screen' or 'out front' doing the face-to-face work. Their 'ownership' of the case would be exactly the same in both situations however.

The creation of such groups does not imply that decisions made by groups are necessarily superior to decisions made by individual social workers. The advantage of corporate decision-making is that decisions become corporate property and, as such, awesome and often disabling decisions are lifted from the shoulders of individuals or teams with a consequent reduction in the degree of stress they experience.

It should follow from this that the bad practice we identified above would be diminished, if not eradicated. Staff would be less able to opt for conservative non-intervention, or dumping, because staff working with a young offender, for example, would be required by the administrative gate, closed across the pathway to custody, to search for alternative placements and to devise an SIR which argues for such a placement. While not eradicating conflict between professionals, the mandating process would allow for the resolution of differences and provide a forum in which a far less personalised discussion of options could take place.

A policy framework

Diana Robbins (1989) argues that there is often considerable confusion in SSDs about policy. Too often *statements of philosophy, policies* and *strategies* are all jumbled up together. She states:

> There are ... examples of authorities attempting to bring together underlying principles, policies and plans for action in one document. In some cases, the definitions are missing, logical links are weak, and the arguments are very difficult to follow. A number are comprehensive and clear, but ultimately too dense and bulky to be of much more practical day-to-day use.

An effective and coherent policy, by contrast, must distinguish clearly between different levels. By way of clarification we have adapted Diana Robbins' example of the levels at which policy statements may be made about child protection in Table 8.1.

Table 8.1: Levels of policy statements

	Level	Statement
Values, beliefs, principles	Philosophy	All children should be free from violence
Aims, objectives	Policy	To reduce the incidence of child physical abuse
	Strategy	Intensive social work with families; community development; inter-agency co-operation
Detailed plans for implementation	Tactics	Step-up house calls; participate in local residents groups
Practice guidance for daily work	Procedures	Reasons for fear of abuse should be discussed with manager at once

It is evident that policy formulation may proceed from a number of different levels. There are, for example, advantages in starting from a statement of philosophy in that the abstract and general nature of such a statement means that it is likely to attract broad-based support. Starting here, policy can be constructed deductively as the implications of the philosophy are fleshed out at the levels of policy, strategy and tactics. On the other hand, the more abstract and general the starting point, the more difficult it will be to develop an appropriate practice. We must remember that in social work, many things which do not work in theory nonetheless work in practice.

Alternatively we might attempt to arrive at policy inductively, by working towards a situation in which our face-to-face work is codified into tactics and procedures and its implication elaborated into a policy which is legitimated by a philosophy. The problem with this approach is that by legitimatising 'what is' this can militate against necessary changes. In fact the process pursued within the standing conference was a dialectical one in which there was an interplay between the different levels of policy formulation.

In this connection Robbins notes that the most important aspect of policy statements is the impact that the process of their formulation has on the culture and ethos of the practice of social work in an organisation. As Chris Gostick notes in Chapter 9 the standing conference set out to promote just such a process in which a discourse rather than a prescription could be developed.

If we bring together some of the problems and issues already discussed with directions for policy change identified here and elsewhere in this volume we can begin to develop a rough sketch of what a policy for effective work with marginalised young people would look like.

Philosopy

All marginalised young people in the borough have the right to a personalised service which meets the highest professional standards.

Policy

The philosophical statement could be articulated via the following type of policy committments.

1. All marginalised young people should have the right for their disturbed or dangerous behaviour to be accepted and worked with sensitively, non-punitively and consistently.
2. All marginalised young people should be allowed to play a full part in determining the outcome of significant life

decisions taken about them while they are in the care of the authority.
3. All marginalised young people should have the right to the maximum degree of self-determination commensurate with their own physical or mental well-being and any demonstrable risk they pose to other people.
4. All marginalised young people should therefore have a right of appeal against any decision taken by staff of the authority to initiate proceedings which may result in confinement in secure accommodation.
5. All marginalised young people should have available to them whatever social treatments or interventions have been demonstrated to be effective in responding to the problems they are experiencing.

Strategy

Policy commitment 1. could then be broken down into strategies like the following:

(a) Devise and distribute codes of practice for the operation of the gates in the authority's decision-making.
(b) Establish a system of mandate groups for all young people in care or deemed to be at serious emotional or physical risk within the authority's geographical area.
(c) Minimise the use of secure accommodation by pushing decision-making up to member level.
(d) Abandon the minimum cover residential staffing strategy in favour of one based on professional tasks to be undertaken in line with the care plan agreed with the young person and her/his mandate group.
(e) Revise performance indicators to reflect the complexity of the professional task to be undertaken rather than the occupancy or use levels of facilities.
(f) Develop a staff training and consultancy network available to workers in all settings which focuses on, amongst other things, the management of disturbed and threatening behaviour.
(g) Produce realistic estimates of repair and refurbishment costs in residential establishments for borough surveyors department and consult with the Director to get the issue of devolved resource management onto the agenda of the social services committee.

Procedures

Some of the day-to-day procedures would appear in the code of practice for the operation of gates. The other major points of reference would be the contract negotiated between the worker and her or his mandate group and the group consultation and supervision of the practice conducted in the space created by the mandate.

Such a policy, were it to be developed might begin to reverse the present situation in which, all too often, young people on the periphery of the family, the school and the justice system are propelled further towards the margins by social work intervention or its absence. If the attempt to develop a framework for policy is about anything, therefore, it is about enabling us to deliver an optimal service to young people in crisis.

References

Parker H 1989 *Unmasking the Magistrates*. Open University Press
Pitts J 1990 *Working with Young Offenders*. BASW/Macmillan
Robbins D 1989 *Child Care Policy: Putting It in Writing*. HMSO

9 Managing change and improving services for young people in crisis

Chris Gostick

> This chapter considers the role of collaborative research in the process of improving the quality and sensitivity of social services. It addresses the changed relationship between managers and practitioners which collaborative research requires and throws out a challenge to researchers, and groups charged with monitoring the quality of welfare services, to listen to, and allow practitioners to participate in the identification and definition of the problems they will be called upon to solve.

All social welfare organisations are facing a tide of major change and uncertainty; a tide which has been growing for a number of years. In social services departments this tide increasingly shows signs of engulfing everything we have been working to create over the past years. Whilst it is clearly necessary to respond to these changes it is equally important to retain clear values and a sharp perspective, so that we can both respond and change for the better on the one hand, whilst ensuring those key values are retained on the other. The issue therefore is not about whether to change, but how to ensure that change is a positive and sustaining experience, rather than a negative or dispiriting one.

These pressures for change are coming from a variety of directions. They come from new legislation; from new political and economic concerns about social welfare; from the changing values of society itself; as well as from staff who are becoming better trained and who understandably expect a more effective voice in the way services are planned and delivered; and from clients, carers and users, who want to share more actively in the processes that surround the development and delivery of the services they require.

Voluntary organisations are also becoming the partners of local authorities in direct service delivery on the one hand, whilst increasingly advocating the rights of individuals to be more active and challenging to the ways of bureaucracy on the other. And

Managing change and improving services

whilst we in social services departments, health and education authorities may be willing, and sometimes indeed even eager, to change, we are still confronted by traditional and bureaucratic local government finance, accounting and personnel systems, seemingly impervious to the demands of devolved resource management and the flexible service responses, outlined by Sir Roy Griffiths and the Audit Commission, and now set out in the emerging new legislation and policy guidance.

In his report *Agenda for Action* Sir Roy Griffith emphasised the role of client and carer as somewhat passive recipients of care packages. Lady Wagner and her committee on the other hand placed much more emphasis on the need to empower and enfranchise users so that they can become more active in the creation of the social provision they require. The response to these different views in the new legislation and the draft guidance from the Department of Health is still confused, but over the next few years it will be the responsibility of managers and practitioners within social services departments to confront these issues and to begin to develop responses.

At its best, the new legislation requires professional staff to see clients not just as fellow citizens, but as partners in the process of service development and delivery. No one would disagree with the rightness of that approach, but underlying it is the rather simplistic idea that through some process of calm negotiation agreement can be achieved. Yet anyone faced with the demands of a turbulent and angry adolescent; a reluctant family; an exhausted foster parent; a disappointed school or irate magistrate cannot fail to agree with Edith Sitwell that there is no truth, only a variety of points of view. Yet someone, somewhere, somehow, has to take a decision, decide what it is that must be done, and ensure that it is done. It is the responsibility of senior managers and elected members to ensure that a framework for such decisions exists; and to be supportive and facilitative to the process of implementation, in an effort to ensure that professional practice is continually developed and improved.

Whilst improving practice does not often make the headlines, there is mounting evidence that over the past few years social services staff have become increasingly concerned with the pursuit of excellence, particularly in services for children and young people. These ideals are supported both by developing skills in effective practice and increasing knowledge derived from research in this country and elsewhere, just at a time when the necessary resources to respond more effectively are no longer available, and indeed show signs of declining.

These then, are the issues now facing managers, practitioners and policy makers in social services agencies, as well as researchers and teachers in the social sciences. Taken together they make substantial, sustained and rapid change in the way we work and respond, and in the organisations that we create, both inevitable and imperative. This recognition of the need for change is not new, research and evaluation studies have frequently highlighted the gap between policy objectives and local practice, and between professionally agreed standards and actual services, particularly within the personal social services. Having identified this 'implementation gap', the challenge is how to create a bridge across the divide.

The crucial problem facing managers in all human service organisations, not just social services departments, is how to achieve change of any sort. This contrasts with manufacturing industry, for example, where to change the product you simply install new machinery and retrain the operators, or so it appears to an outsider. No doubt the reality is a little different. But people are both the product and the process of human service organisations, and we instinctively seek the stability and reassurance of the familiar, so that bringing about change is inevitably uncomfortable, difficult and not infrequently ineffective. Whilst this should be seen as more a reflection of the difficulties of the process, than the obduracy of the individuals involved (who have invariably been recruited into human service organisations because of a commitment to the very services the changes are designed, or at least intended, to improve), it is still a powerful force for inertia.

It is this potential inertia which needs to be addressed as part of the process of understanding, initiating and achieving change. It can take many forms: in social services, for example, it is sometimes called professional judgement; in the universities it often travels under the colours of academic freedom; and in the health services it can appear as clinical autonomy. Each in its own way is an understandable response; a reaffirmation of faith in known skills, competence, experience and training; as well as a commitment to existing values. It is also symptomatic of the fear of the new and the unknown. Nevertheless, each remains a form of restrictive practice that must be confronted if managers and practitioners are to bring about change, and improve the relationship between resource input and service outcome, which is the crucial measure of service effectiveness.

In this process of confronting and achieving change we have not always been helped by the teachers and researchers who shape the institutional, intellectual and theoretical environment in which practice now operates. Research in particular has not systematically addressed itself to the very real problems being faced by managers and front line staff, even though some of it has been of very real importance. Much research is still presented in ways that are inpenetrable, inaccessible, or incomprehensible to hard pressed managers and practitioners, although the recent attempt by the Department of Health to present key research findings in child care within a local practice framework (*Social Work Decisions in Child Care* HMSO 1985) is a salutatory demonstration of how effective research findings can be presented with a little more thought and effort. Similar work is now urgently needed in other areas of concern.

Even more alarming is the way in which much important research is frequently ignored by professional training courses, as is the need to teach the basic principles of research, so that practitioners can both use research findings and critically evaluate its approach and conclusions. Sadly, despite a few valuable exceptions, there is still no recognition of the need to equip practitioners with the necessary skills to evaluate their own practice, and to undertake small scale research reviews of their own work; whereas medical training (and increasingly nursing) is considered essentially incomplete without a major element of research. In such circumstances it is hardly surprising that research findings normally have as little impact on practice as do policy initiatives or management directives from on high. It is not simply stubbornness on the part of practitioners to be uninterested or unresponsive to alternative approaches, but the inability of researchers, teachers and managers to involve them in a process which allows them to evaluate critically their own practice in a safe manner, as a first step in the process of exploring more effective ways of responding to the very real problems that they face.

As a researcher I was invariably surprised and disappointed by the lack of enthusiasm with which my earnest reports were greeted by practitioners, and I begin to see the same anxiety creeping into the Social Services Inspectorate as they issue their reports in ever greater abundance, but with noticeably little impact. And I have an equal anxiety that the new independent inspection units now being established in each local authority under the Care in the Community directives will be similarly unresponsive unless their evaluation activities can be much more closely linked with practice, and their orientation turned towards the achievement of quality, rather than the policing of policy and regulations.

It is no easy task to achieve change in the organisation, management and quality of human care of the sort that is increasingly required. We are invariably faced with inadequate resources to undertake the process of change, and there are always equally pressing issues requiring attention elsewhere. But such changes are achievable, and I maintain that we owe it to clients and users, as well as to ourselves as professionals, to ensure that we both bring about change and continually strive to improve practice. But it is increasingly clear that such changes and improvements can only be achieved by collaboration between practitioners, managers, teachers and users, each with an equal role and equal commitment to the process. I believe that the collaborative processes outlined in this book begin to show a successful way to confront those issues, and to achieve improvements in a positive manner.

These are large claims to make for the comparatively modest achievements we have reported, but they are based on previous work which clearly suggests that significant changes can be achieved in a positive and stimulating way by the joint application of research and practice skills, by involving users wherever possible, and by looking to improvements in process and practice as outcomes, rather than a somewhat grandiose research report. Just as work has to be a positive and enjoyable experience to be effective, so change can only be achieved with a positive commitment to its outcome, based on a clear understanding of the shortcoming of existing services, practices or policies, and the ways in which each might be improved.

The central difference with this collaborative approach is that it reverses the traditional role of practitioners and managers in the change process. Managers no longer control the outcome, but become participants in the process. As a result much of the discomfort and uncertainty of change is removed from frontline staff and redirected towards managers, who are in many ways better placed to absorb those anxieties and to respond more positively. I believe that the activities reported in this book begin to demonstrate beyond any reasonable doubt the enormous importance of adopting a collaborative process, in which those people with the necessary conceptual and methodological skills derived from research can assist managers and practitioners to reassess their activities, by providing a framework within which existing services can be reviewed and evaluated, and potential alternatives begin to be developed.

This is neither a difficult nor an esoteric process, but it does take time and commitment, and an ability amongst all those involved in the process, whether they be managers, practitioners or researchers, to be able to face up to difficult conclusions and to think creatively about possible alternatives. Such a process should, of course, become central to the way that we plan, develop and deliver all our services, and not be regarded as a discrete exercise looking at a particular service, delivered in a particular way at a particular time.

Nonetheless, whilst this is a comparatively modest start, it clearly signals a new approach to the evaluation of services, and the need for partnership between managers, practitioners and researchers

Managing change and improving services

based on a shared commitment to the improvement of practice, and the quality of service to users. If such a response can be achieved then this modest beginning really does represent the possibility of a move towards a new era of collaboration, and some hope of achieving the needs orientated approach to services increasingly being required by both government policy and by current practice and professional values. That, of course, is a far less modest goal, and a much more worthy objective. On the basis of the work reported in this book, we believe the achievement of that possibility is now within our grasp.